"As the title [of this book suggests, a gospel-]centered approach is, in the long run, the most effective way to combat sin and addiction. Any resource, like this one by Paul O'Brien, which helps us fight our sinful compulsions by means of the gospel of Jesus Christ is one I recommend."

– DR. DONALD S. WHITNEY,

Professor of Biblical Spirituality and Associate Dean at The Southern Baptist Theological Seminary, and author or Spiritual Disciplines of the Christian Life and Praying the Bible.

"Paul is a genuine man of faith who has dedicated his life to Jesus and his calling. As a former heroin addict who was mentored by Paul, I had the privilege to witness his passion for Christ and his desire to help people through God's word. This book shows that same passion."

– RICKY UPTON,

Louisville, KY

"*Gospel-Centered War* is for those who struggle with life-dominating sin and for those who counsel them. Instead of simply addressing behavior modification, Paul O'Brien gets to the heart of the matter. This book addresses the issues that provide freedom from destructive, self-defeating behaviors by helping the reader understand how God can change their heart and passions. Read it, devour it, and then be changed from the inside out."

– PASTOR MIKE WILSON,

Lincoln Heights Baptist Church, Mansfield, Ohio

VERITAS PRESS

Veritas Press exists to glorify God by creating truth-centered resources for human flourishing.

Other Veritas Press resources:

Date Different: A Short (but real) Conversation on Dating, Sex, and Marriage for Teenagers (and their parents)

Friendship Redeemed: How the Gospel Changes Friendships to Something Greater

Friendship Established: The 'Genesis' of True Friendships

Follow VP on Twitter @Veritas_Press

Purchase at TheVeritasNetwork.org

Gospel-Centered War
Finding Freedom from Enslaving Sin

Paul O'Brien

Veritas Press
2016

Copyright ©2015 by Paul O'Brien

All rights reserved. No part of this publication may be reproduced in any form without written permission from the author. Made and designed in the United States of America.

ISBN-13: 978-0692684863
ISBN-10: 0692684867

Scripture quotations are from The Holy Bible, English Standard Version® (ESV®), copyright © 2001 by Crossway, a publishing ministry of Good News Publishers. Used by permission. All rights reserved.

The brief excerpts from Alcoholic Anonymous are reprinted with permission of A.A. World Services, Inc. Permission to reprint these excerpts does not mean that A.A.W.S. has reviewed or approved the contents of this publication, or that A.A.W.S. necessarily agrees with the views expressed herein. A.A. it is not a religious program - it is a spiritual program. Thus, A.A. is not affiliated or allied with any sect, denomination, or specific religious belief.

Veritas Press Supervising Editor: Greg Gibson

Cover & Layout Design by Mathew B. Sims
www.MathewBryanSims.com

To My Comrades and Son, Uriah

The gospel-centered war is difficult, and it is increasingly filled with landmines. But the fight is worth it. So fight on!

Remember, Satan is the great deceiver, and he's good at what he does. Don't listen to him. Keep God's truth always before you; it's a shining light that will light the dark slippery paths.

Athletes show amazing self-control. They do it to get a perishable prize, but we "compete" for an imperishable prize. So do not act like your discipline and self-control is pointless, it's not! But keep yourself under control. There is a great prize laid up for you in heaven.
– 1 Corinthians 9:24-27

TABLE OF CONTENTS

Introduction   9

Part One: Help for the Helper

1 How to Help	15
2 We Need Compassionate Hearts	25
3 Jesus Can Relate to Addicts	31
4 Broken Cisterns or Abounding Streams?	35
5 It is a Heart Problem	51

Part Two: The Transformation Process

6 What Forms and (Re)forms You?	63
7 Be Mindful of Your Mind	77
8 The Fighthyperlink of Faith	89

Part Three: Transformational Steps

9 Don't Listen to Lies	101
10 Remember, Sin is Not Good	113
11 Hello, my name is ___ and I am ~~an Addict~~ Transformed	137
12 Be Transformed by Gospel Motivation	147
13 Be Transformed by Community	153
14 Be Transformed by Radical Measures	165
15 Be Transformed by Worship	173

16 Be Transformed by a New Consuming Passion 185

(Not a) Conclusion 191

About the Author 193

INTRODUCTION

It is a graphic scene, depicted in the most vivid way. A recent celebrated movie shows the character smiling in glee as he takes his own life. This depiction is sad, yet we see it week-in and week-out. The movie is The Return of the King and the character is Gollom. Formerly known as Sméagol when he was a regular Hobbit, Gollom was corrupted, enslaved by a ring. His infatuation with the ring started slowly (a weekend here and there) but ended desperately. Gollom loved and hated the ring. He was torn -- he wanted to be free from the ring, and yet relentlessly pursued it.

At the end of the movie, Gollom finally has, as he calls the ring, "my precious." But in getting the ring he has destroyed himself and everyone, indeed, everything around him. Even still, the ring remains his "precious." Gollom's last scene is one of great joy (for him). Gollom fights Frodo over the ring, another character that is nearly destroyed completely by the ring. Gollom is fierce. He

INTRODUCTION

wants the ring at any price. He bites off Frodo's finger and rejoices over his plunder. He embraces his cruel master as his beloved friend. He falls, seemingly, blissfully in the lava and as he sinks he rejoices that he has comfort from pain, he has everything, he has his "precious." Then he sinks and he and his "precious" are gone forever.

This scenario plays out similarly to the climax and conclusion of far too many addiction stories. It is heartbreaking to see people enraptured by their cruel master and executioner. However, there is reason for hope; hope that is found in the Bible and the good news of Jesus Christ. You may be thinking, "I have never seen the word 'addiction' in the Bible, so how does it speak to the subject of addiction, specifically substance abuse?" There are many paradigms in Scripture that apply.[1] This is not to say that any passage on one of these subjects can be blandly applied to addictions. Instead, these paradigms must be faithfully taught and brought to life for the counselee.

In this book, I have written so that the counselee and the counselor can both read and receive help. By taking this approach, I hope that individuals who are reading this for

---

[1] See passages referring to sin, enslavement, idolatry, adultery, whoring, lust, drunkenness, etc. For instance, on drunkenness see: Prov. 20:1; 23:29-35; Is. 5:11-12, 22; Luke 21:34; Rom. 13:13; 1 Cor. 5:11; 6:9-10; Gal. 5:19-21; Eph. 5:18

INTRODUCTION

themselves will find it helpful and use the material to help others. We are all people in need of change, helping people in need of change.[2]

The idea for this book came out of a desire to help my friends who've struggled with substance abuse, particularly heroin. I've broadened the subject to include the enslaving sins of substance abuse and pornography.

As a Christian, I am offering a biblical, rather than a clinical approach to overcoming sin. Above all, it is my desire to see people transformed by God's radical grace and be set free as they encounter, and then grow to know and love the LORD God and His Son, Jesus Christ. God loves us in spite of our sins and has the power to transform us into the image of Jesus.

PRAYER:

God, help all who are now caught in the snare of enslaving sin, we ask. You are a good Father and we come to You, asking that You will set us free. Lord, change us. Help us. We ask this in Jesus' Name and by Your Spirit. And we ask this that You may be glorified LORD. Amen.

---

[2] See the subtitle of Paul David Tripp's helpful book, *Instruments in the Redeemer's Hands: People in Need of Change Helping People in Need of Change* (Phillipsburg, NJ: P&R Publishing, 2002).

PART ONE: HELP FOR THE HELPER

"We urge you, brothers, admonish the idle, encourage the fainthearted, help the weak, be patient with them all."
– 1 Thessalonians 5:14

"Reprove, rebuke, and exhort, with complete patience and teaching."
– 2 Timothy 4:2

1
HOW TO HELP

"The incomplete joys of this world can never satisfy [man's] heart. Man is the only creature to exhibit both a natural disgust for existence and an overwhelming desire to exist: he despises life and fears nothingness."[3]
– Alexis de Tocqueville, *Democracy in America*

"I still haven't found what I'm looking for…"
– Bono

Seeking to help others overcome their enslaving sins is complicated because people are complicated and everyone's story is unique. The process is dynamic and requires the truths of Scripture and help from the Holy Spirit. The counsel you give always requires

---

[3] Alexis de Tocqueville, *Democracy in America* (New York: Literary Classics of the United States, Inc., 2004), Vol. 1, Part 2, 342.

nuancing (cf. Acts 20:35; Rom. 15:1; 1 Cor. 15:1; 1 Thess. 5:14; 2 Tim. 4:2).

The first step is to consider your view of man because everything you say and do will flow directly from your that perspective. Do you believe, as is common in our American culture, that men and women are essentially good and that the goal of life is to realize our potential? If so, the core problem is obstacles that get in the way of people expressing all of their goodness.

Or, do you believe what the Bible says: that men and women are made in the image of God, but because of original sin, our natures have been corrupted. We are tempted to sin and the resulting consequences create problems in how we think, feel, and act. However, there is reason to hope because Jesus Christ came to earth to die for our sins and to bring us new life. With this view, which is the one I take in this book, the problem is who or what we worship because our worship determines how we think and act.

> *If you are going to help someone, you need to know what is wrong and how it can be fixed. You go to your auto mechanic because he can determine why your car is malfunctioning and get it running again. Any trustworthy*

HOW TO HELP

perspective on personal change must do the same. It must correctly diagnose what is wrong with people and what is necessary for them to change.

This is where our culture gets it completely wrong. In rejecting a biblical view of people, the world eliminates any hope of answering the 'what is wrong?' question accurately. And if it wrongly answers this question, how can it possibly provide a proper solution?[4]

As we seek help or seek to help others we don't want to whitewash the situation because that will lead to superficial solutions.[5] If we whitewash the situation and say it is not that bad, *we* are not that bad, we will miss the answer. We know, we *all* know, there is a problem. Some of us even expect that the problem is us. In fact, it is reported by different sources that *The London Times* once asked its readers, 'What is the greatest problem in the world?' A famous novelist responded succinctly:

---

[4] Paul David Tripp, *Instruments in the Redeemer's Hands*, 9. Similarly, Sam Williams has said, "It goes without saying that a prerequisite for defining a disorder is a prior apprehension of the proper order" ("Toward a Theology of Emotion" in *The Southern Baptist Journal of Theology*, 7/4 [Winter 2003]: 66).

[5] John R. W. Stott, *The Message of Ephesians* (Downers Grove: InterVarsity Press, 1979), 85.

HOW TO HELP

I am.
Sincerely yours,
George MacDonald

Most people, however, do not want to admit that there is anything wrong. In essence, modern man wants to put various Band-Aids on people's and societies' problems. But people and thus the society in which they live are dead. Thus, the solution that the secular world offers obviously comes far short. It's like someone's head just plopped off and people are saying everything will be okay. We'll just grab the gauze.

People! It is *not* okay. This *is* a big deal!

Many people are sadly blind to the reality of our situation. They don't know what "sickness" we have, what "healthy" looks like, or what the "cure" is. They can't answer these questions because their worldview does not allow for it. It is the inevitable result of that worldview. It is odd or foolish, is it not, that that system of thought says there is no problem but yet they are trying to fix something (unhappiness, addiction, etc.) but they do not know for what they aim. They have no model for fixed. That is, they don't know what truly healthy is. And without an ideal of what is broken, and what fixed is, it is hard to do much of anything.

Scripture tells us that we are broken, desperately broken, and it even very

HOW TO HELP

unpopularly calls us sinful6 (cf. Gen. 6:5; 8:21; Ps. 51:5; Jer. 13:23; Jn. 6:44; Rom. 3:10-11; 5:12ff; 8:7-9; 1 Cor. 2:14). Yet, it also tells us what fixed looks like; namely, Jesus (e.g. Col. 1:15). However, it doesn't leave us there. It doesn't just give us a picture of broken and a picture of fixed, it gives us a bridge to cross the gulf that has been made. This bridge is the cross. The cross where the "fixed" One died for the broken ones so that they could be fixed (2 Cor. 5:21); fixed once-and-for-all in the site of God. And progressively fixed until they finally know what it means to be right and whole (Rom. 8:29; 1 Cor. 15:49; 2 Cor. 3:18).[7]

The truth of Scripture is hard. But who expects the answer to a problem not to be hard; especially of this caliber? We are broken. We need fixed. That is plain enough.

---

[6] "Human sinfulness is an abominable breach in the meaningful fabric of the universe, the active increasing of a kind of mysterious black hole in the evaluative center of human life, the heart.... Humans are born with a psychopathological condition that the Bible calls 'sin'" (Eric L. Johnson, *Foundations of Soul Care: A Christian Psychology Proposal* [Downers Grove: InterVarsity Press, 2007], 462).

[7] Eric Johnson has said, "As the Real Man... Christ is the human ideal, so he is the Form toward which human beings are supposed to be moving" (*Foundations for Soul Care,* 28-29). Thus, sanctification (which is true psychological health) "entails an increasing conformity to the image of Christ—the ideal Form of human life—it must also include an inward dimension, affecting the depth structures and activities of the heart..., and encompassing affective dispositions, attitudes, motives, loves and hates, and character traits (i.e., virtues)" (Ibid., 47).

HOW TO HELP

When I was a young boy I drew lots of pictures of people with gaping holes in either their eye sockets or chest. This was to communicate a feeling I had and realized all people have. It is a feeling, a longing, a need for more. A need for meaning. I realized that humanity worships all sorts of things that leave them empty. And I began to see that we need to redirect our longing to the LORD.

This need or thirst is quite satisfactorily explained by Scripture. It tells us that originally everything was good (Gen. 1:31) and that man had undisturbed friendship with God. But, sadly, not for very long. Chaos and curse ensued from sin in the Garden. Separation from God, each other, and creation. The world, and all in it, left groaning for redemption (Rom. 8:22).

The whole of humanity has a vacuum in their heart and that is it. It sucks in all it can, as Calvin famously said, our mind is like a production line spitting out idol after idol. Many other voices echo this same truth. And we all realize that America, with its unprecedented wealth, still hasn't truly lived it's dream. "The incomplete joys of this world can never satisfy [man's] heart. Man is the only creature to exhibit both a natural disgust

HOW TO HELP

for existence and an overwhelming desire to exist: he despises life and fears nothingness."[8]

A consistent theme woven through many C.S. Lewis books is the theme of longing. Lewis very often reminds us that all the beauty we take in is actually a mere faint echo of what was and will yet be. Our fondest memories and sweetest moments are but traces. And all our deepest thirsts and desires can be joyfully satisfied. But not yet. Not here. We have a desire for heaven and full-communion with God but it is yet to be filled. And so we ache.

We can all relate to yearning for something more. We can relate to Bono, who still hasn't found what he's looking for. Scripture certainly echoes this truth as well: the human heart is a perpetual vacuum. Yet, the Bible also gives us the answer. Jesus said, Come to me and I will give you rest (Matt. 11:28 see also Ps. 42:1-2; 63:1; Is. 12:3; 44:3; 55:1-3; Jn. 4:14; 7:37). Peter tells us that we are waiting for the new heavens and a new earth in which righteousness dwells (2 Pet. 3:11-13). We are waiting for our every longing to be met as we meet our Lord face to face. We are waiting for what was marred in creation to be restored.

---

[8] Alexis de Tocqueville, *Democracy in America* (New York: Literary Classics of the United States, Inc., 2004), Vol. 1, Part 2, 342.

HOW TO HELP

Jesus, by His wrath absorbing sacrifice, enables a way for restored relationship with God. Jesus destroyed the work of the devil (1 John 3:8; Col. 2:20) and is making all things new (Rev. 21:5). We eagerly await the redemption of our bodies (Rom. 8:23; 1 Cor. 15:49) when we will finally know the peace and rest that Scripture so often talks about and we so often long for. "Beloved, we are God's children now, and what we will be has not yet appeared; but we know that when He appears we shall be like Him, because we shall see Him as He is" (1 Jn. 3:2).

The problem is bigger then we can imagine but the solution is better then we can imagine. God the Son came lived and died for those who turned away from Him. He came to reorient our worship away from paths of death to the path of joy and life. A path that leads to restored friendship with Him.

This book is titled "Gospel-Centered War" because finding freedom from enslaving sin is war. But we don't fight the war alone. And our motivation is not merely our own but is grounded in the surpassing worth of the gospel.

TAKE AWAY

- Do you know, deeply, intimately know, you're broken? Do you feel the

HOW TO HELP

weight of your sin? This is a prerequisite to being "fixed."
- What sin/idol are you trying to fill your gaping black hole with?
- Think about your sin. Think about how much you *don't* deserve God's grace. Pray that God would help you know the weight of your sin. Then pray that God would help you know that the weight of your sin is cast upon Christ. This is important because those who have been forgiven much, love much (cf. Lk. 7:47).

Think about the vicious cycle of addiction. Think about your desire. Yet, think how it never *truly* fulfills. Our desire is broken. This world is broken. What this tells us is that we have a desire within us that this world cannot fulfill. We long for a *new* earth in which righteousness dwells (2 Peter 3:13).

2
WE NEED COMPASSIONATE HEARTS

As we seek to help those with addiction problems, we must not forget the important qualification of compassion. Without compassion what otherwise would have been helpful will be self-righteous. What example do we have of compassion? What biblical model can we think of? None other than Jesus Himself! Jesus had abundant riches in heaven yet He left heaven for us and became poor that through His poverty we might become rich (2 Cor. 8:9). In Philippians, we are told to look not only to our own interests, but also the interests of others (2:4). Why should we do this? Because Jesus, who is God, humbled

WE NEED COMPASSIONATE HEARTS

Himself and took the form of a servant to die for us (vv. 6-8). Our attitude should be the same as Christ Jesus' (v. 5).

We know from the Gospels that Jesus had compassion on people.[9] He was even criticized by the religious leaders of the day because of the type of people that He reached out to and helped (cf. Matt. 9:9-13; 11:19; 21:31-32; Mk. 2:15-17; Lk. 3:12-14; 5:29-32; 7:36-50; 15; 19:1-10 for example). He ate with tax collectors even though they would cheat and steal from people (Matthew, who wrote the Gospel of Matthew, was previously a tax collector [Matt. 9:9-13]!). He talked to Gentiles who were basically unacceptable foreigners to many people. Jesus ministered to prostitutes and the friends that were closest to Him were not the religious elite but humble smelly fishermen. If we are to minister compassionately, we must imitate Jesus.

He reached out and literally touched lepers (Matt. 8:2-4; Mark 1:40-44; Lk. 5:12-16). Lepers were people with a severe skin disease. They had to call out "unclean, unclean" when they saw people (cf. Lev. 13:45-46), and Jesus touched them! When

---

[9] Eric L. Johnson has similarly pointed out that "scriptural teaching leads us to infer that God is especially committed to those who have psychological damage and desirous of improving their well-being (Mt 9:11-13; 11:19; 18:6; Lk 6:20; 1 Cor 1:26-28; 2 Cor 4:7; Jas 2:5)" (*Foundations of Soul Care*, 473).

WE NEED COMPASSIONATE HEARTS

Jesus walked up to, let alone talked to and touched, the leper, his followers, to say nothing of the religious leaders, would have been shocked and scandalized. Yet, what is Jesus' response? Did He turn away? Did He tell the leper to stay back? No. Jesus was filled with compassion (Mark 1:41). He cared for the outcast. He loved the unlovely even when it was the unpopular thing. Loathsome leprosy is not beyond Jesus' loving touch.

Think of the biggest outcasts in today's society—whether to you its addicts, illegal immigrants, poor people, unattractive people, so-called "white trash," or whoever you think of—they are not outcasts to Jesus. He loves them. He reaches for them. No one is past His reach. No one is too sick for Him.

One of the most amazing things that we learn from the cleansing of the leper is that outsiders and addicts can experience the transforming touch of the Lord Jesus.[10] He is there and He cares. You may not feel like you deserve His touch, you might feel dirty, but Jesus cares. He reaches out to outcasts, to the filthy, to you and me!

The Church, taking her cues from Jesus, must do the same. Jesus loved the seemingly unlovely (again, you and me) and so must we. It is the very essence of Christianity to touch

---

[10] See Darrell L. Bock, *Luke* in The NIV Application Commentary (Grand Rapids: Zondervan Publishing House, 1996), 165.

WE NEED COMPASSIONATE HEARTS

the untouchable, to love the unlovable, to forgive the unforgivable. Jesus did and so must we.

So, are *you* reaching? If we define lepers as those who are isolated, unwanted, the outcasts of society then who are the "lepers" who live around you today? Who are the "lepers" in your sphere of influence?

As we seek to minister compassionately, we must remember the gospel. For those that didn't know, we were *all* once vile sinners, a.k.a. addicts, but we have been washed, made holy, and declared righteous in the name of the Lord Jesus Christ (cf. 1 Cor. 6:9-11).

We must understand that "none is righteous, no, not one" (see e.g. Rom. 3:10), and this includes you, me, the substance abuser, and porn user. We are the "leper." We *all* have sinned. Yet through the redemption that is in Christ Jesus we can be declared righteous by God's grace (Rom. 3:23).

We may not have the same addiction but we all have the sin problem. No, all sin does not look the same and does not have the same consequences (cf. 1 Cor. 6:18; Prov. 5:7-14) but it is all sin against a holy God. The ground is level at the foot of the cross. May we realize that we ourselves are sinners, even "the chief of sinners," and say with Paul, "by the grace of God I am what I am" (1 Cor. 15:10). May we

WE NEED COMPASSIONATE HEARTS

not be like the prideful Pharisee that puts himself over others (Lk. 18:11 cf. 13-14).

The loving and reaching grace of our humble and exalted Lord should create new Kingdom communities that transform.

TAKE AWAY

- Are you reaching out to others and loving them?
- Is compassionately serving "lepers" out of your comfort zone?
- Do you know that you, yourself, are sinful and not beyond the sins of another? Are you puffed up? Do you think you're better than others because you've never struggled with X, Y, or Z? You're not! Know that it's only by God's grace that you're saved, that you're... anything.
- Meditate on Christ and what He's done for you (cf. 2 Cor. 8:9; Phil. 2:3-8) and be transformed into His image.
- Do you recognize your own "leprosy"?
- Dear brother or sister, picture yourself in the worst state that you've ever been in. Now picture Jesus' loving hand reaching out to you in the midst of it to cleanse and pull you out of it.

3
JESUS CAN RELATE TO ADDICTS

Does anyone care? Can anyone relate to what I'm going through?

Addicts suffer physically, socially, emotionally, and spiritually. The book of Hebrews tells us that Jesus was tempted just like we are and yet never sinned (Heb. 4:15; 7:26; 1 Peter 2:22; 1 Jn. 3:5). Actually, Satan himself tempted Jesus. Jesus hadn't eaten anything for forty whole days and He was in the middle of nowhere and that is when Satan struck. He came to Jesus in His weakest state. Yet, Jesus did not give in.

You may think, "Well then, if Jesus was so successful when He was tempted then surely He cannot relate to me. I always mess up." The book of Hebrews tells us Jesus *can* relate to us. It says He is able to sympathize with

JESUS CAN RELATE TO ADDICTS

our weaknesses (Heb. 4:15; cf. 5:1-10) and it is says that He is able to help those that are tempted (Heb. 2:18). Yes, Jesus never sinned but He can relate, He was tempted by the father of lies himself. He, in fact, faced a bigger challenge than you, He *is* sympathetic!

Jesus Himself suffered in all these ways. Jesus suffered great physical pain. Many addicts crave food, a substance, sex, or some such thing. As I said, Jesus fasted for *forty days*, He knew what it was to have physical cravings. Jesus suffered a terrible bloody death on the cross. Jesus can relate to physical suffering.

He suffered socially. He was not welcomed in His own town—He who dwelt in heaven! People mocked where He was from. "Can anything good come from there?" they would say. Jesus was not physically attractive (Is. 53:2-3), no matter how modern movies portray Him. We know Jesus was physically poor. He Himself said, "Foxes have holes but I have no place to lay my head." People said that He was filled with demons, though He cast out demons. People said He was an illegitimate son. Religious people could not stand Him and were always out to get Him. Jesus who merits eternal praise, indeed the rocks crying out, was mocked by the thief beside Him as He bled on the cross for the sins of a sinful world. Jesus understands social rejection.

JESUS CAN RELATE TO ADDICTS

Jesus felt emotional pain. The shortest verse in the Bible says, "Jesus wept." That is profound. It shows us that Jesus was not some untouchable stoic. He felt grief, He felt pain, more then we can ever understand. He felt emotional pain more acutely, I would argue, because He understood the implications of things better than we can. He had seen, for instance, Adam and Eve in the Garden before the Fall. So, He weeps understanding more than we can how sickening sin and thus death truly is. He wept over Jerusalem. He wept in the garden of Gethsemane. Jesus can relate to our emotional struggles.

Jesus, the Son of God, suffered spiritually. This was His greatest suffering. First, He left heaven and took the form of a man (see Phil. 2:5-8; 2 Cor. 8:9). Second, and worst of all, Jesus bore the wrath of God for us on the cross. Jesus cried from the cross, "My God, my God, why have You forsaken Me?" He was crushed under the wrath of God for us, He was cast out that we might be welcomed in. Jesus drank the cup of God's wrath down to the dregs. So that later we could rejoice with wine in the Garden.

Jesus is everything! And He can truly see and relate to everything you are going through or ever will go through. Not only can He *relate* but He has truly overcome it all. I mean everything! He is victorious. He is at the right hand of God the Father. It is through

JESUS CAN RELATE TO ADDICTS

Jesus that *all things* will be made new. All who place their faith in Jesus will experience the joy that He has merited for them. It is through Jesus that every tear will be wiped dry and every sad face will receive an eternal smile.

TAKE AWAY

- How do you struggle physically, socially, emotionally, spiritually?
- How does Jesus relate to you and your struggles?
- Do you believe Jesus can relate to you? He can! Jesus, God made man, can relate to *you* and your struggles. Not only that, but He cares. He cares about *you* and what you are going through.
- When you're tempted to think no one cares, no one can relate or understand what you're going through, remember Jesus does. Jesus knows, He sees, He cares.
- Take joy and comfort in the fact that Jesus overcame where we fail. And because of His work or sins can be forgiven and we can be made new.
- How can you find comfort knowing that Jesus has suffered greatly in your place?

4
BROKEN CISTERNS OR ABOUNDING STREAM?

BROKEN CISTERNS

"Satiated," do you know what that means? It describes our, and as you will see, Israel's experience.

In Jeremiah chapter two, God announces His indictment on the people of Israel (v. 9). It is in essence putting Israel on trial. What accusation does He bring up against them?

In verses ten and eleven, God says to Israel, there is no precedence for what you are doing. Gentile nations do not even do what you are doing. So what is Israel doing? They are changing their God. The pagan nations do not change their gods and yet God's people have "exchanged" (cf. Rom. 1:23)

BROKEN CISTERNS OR ABOUNDING STREAM?

the glory of God for what does not profit (cf. Jer. 2:4).

Because of Israel's idolatry God says to the heavens "be appalled," be horrified. He is telling the witnesses of the trial to see the nastiness of the crime and be disgusted. The LORD says be shocked. Then, as judgment, God says, "be utterly desolate" (note the connection to v. 13) or exceedingly dried up.[11] This is God saying to Israel, "you trust in other gods thus I will judge you by bringing drought upon your land."

Now we get to the indictment that the LORD announces to the heavens. God condemns His people for committing two crimes. Verse 13 says,

> *"For my people have committed two evils:*
> *they have forsaken me,*
> *the fountain of living waters,*
> *and hewed out cisterns for themselves,*
> *broken cisterns that can hold no water."*

---

[11] What does "being exceedingly dried up" look like? Well, for example, a heroin abuser may inject up to four times a day, withdrawal can occur as early as a few hours after the last use, and it produces drug craving and restlessness. When people turn from God to other devices God gives them up to those things and they in turn wreak havoc on them (cf. Jer. 17:13). Cf. the destroying drug known as Krokodil.

BROKEN CISTERNS OR ABOUNDING STREAM?

First, they have forsaken the one true God. Second, they have pursued other so-called gods.

Israel had hewed out cisterns for themselves. That is, they labored to make wells to drink from. To make a well is not wrong in itself, it makes sense if you need water. However, did Israel have water? Yes, abundant water, living water! To labor for water is illogical when you have water available, especially when you consider that they had clean pure flowing streams of living water available to them. This is the height of folly. Yet it does not stop there. Not only did they labor for water when they had clear access to water but they ended up having *no* water. Their cistern was broken, there was no water, only mud (much like the one Jeremiah was thrown into; see Jer. 38:6).

Imagine you and I go on a jog together. We run all the way to the local high school by the church and all the way back. We finish our jog and you are thirsty. I see you eyeing a puddle in the parking lot so I tell you that we can get some water from the water fountain inside. But before I can get the door unlocked, you're already on your hands and knees sipping up water from the contaminated puddle in the parking lot (one of those puddles that looks like a rainbow because of all the oil in it). What is my thought? Wow, that may be the sickest thing I have ever seen;

BROKEN CISTERNS OR ABOUNDING STREAM?

not only that, it is the stupidest. There is a fountain you could have drunk from! This is, in contemporary terms, what Jeremiah is saying. God's people have forsaken *Him* the creator of all good and turned to nasty and worthless idols. They went after worthlessness and thus became worthless (Jer. 2:5).

The life of sin is a story of someone who has drunk from a broken cistern and drunk deeply from it. This is what life in sin amounts to, a long drink from a broken well. It is like Gollom holding onto the ring. It is holding on to an sin, a cruel master, and calling it "my precious." Sin is ultimately a contaminated puddle that can quench no thirst. So satiated is a fitting word. It means bored from overindulgence.

What is the punishment for those who turn from God, the fountain of living water, to the contaminated, stagnate, and unfulfilling well of sin? Sadly, they become desolate, a worthless wasteland (cf. Jer. 2:5, 12 also Rom. 1). This is, not surprisingly, both a biblical and observational reality.

In Jeremiah's day to hew out a cistern could involve cutting into rock to form a cavity where water could collect. What is wrong with this, you ask, surely we need water. Yes, but this "water" has been abundantly provided, "a fountain of living water." Further, in turning from the true

BROKEN CISTERNS OR ABOUNDING STREAM?

source of life we have turned to that which is broken. A broken cistern could only contain stagnant water, likely containing mosquito larvae. This water would be good for absolutely nothing. Yet when we hew out broken cisterns and forsake the LORD the true source, we have only to drink deeply of filth, the so-called water that will never satisfy. Yet, just like Gollom, we all continue to drink more and more and more, albeit with diminishing returns.[12] What breaks this deadly sin, this deadly worship, this thirst for more?

We must drink from the fountain of *living* water. We must realize what *can* quench our thirst. We may not all realize it but as the deer pants for flowing streams, so pants our soul for God. Our souls thirst for God, for the living God (see Ps. 42:1-2). As Augustine said, our hearts are restless until they rest in Him.

Blaise Pascal, the mathematician and Christian philosopher, says the same type of thing. He asks, What does our desire tell us? It tells us that there was once in us a true happiness of which we now have only the empty trace, which we in vain try to fill from our surroundings. However, all those things

---

[12] Augustine has a good observation regarding the low of diminishing returns. He said the less God allowed him to find pleasure in other things, lesser things, the greater, he knew, was God's goodness to him (From Augustine's autobiography, *Confessions*).

are inadequate. Our infinite emptiness can only be filled by an infinite object, that is, only by God Himself.[13]

Even secular culture recognizes that we have a desire for more. See for example the Rolling Stones' "(I Can't Get No) Satisfaction," Bruce Springsteen's "Hungry Heart," and U2's "I Still Haven't Found What I Am Looking For."

The former guitarist for the heavy rock band Korn, Brian "Head" Welch, said this in his book *Save Me from Myself*:

> *Here I was, the guitarist for one of the biggest rock bands in the world, racking in millions of bucks, and playing huge concerts all over the globe, but I was completely miserable. I didn't understand how a person who had everything he wanted, with millions of dollars in the bank, could be unhappy.[14]*

Later he said that the love of God is what he had really been craving.

> *Take it from me: nothing you chase after on this Earth will satisfy you like a real,*

---

[13] Cf. Blaise Pascal, *Pensées* (148).

[14] Brian Welch, *Save Me from Myself: How I Found God, Quit Korn, Kicked Drugs, and Lived to Tell my Story* (New York: HarperOne, 2007), 2.

BROKEN CISTERNS OR ABOUNDING STREAM?

everyday, intimate relationship with Jesus Christ.

Nothing.

Trust me.

While I was in Korn I had people waiting on me left and right. Anything I wanted, I got. Anywhere I wanted to go, I went. All I had to do was give the word, and it happened. I had the world in the palm of my hand, people; and I have to tell you one last time, there's nothing there. I promise you.

Jesus Christ is the only one that can make you complete.[15]

A desire for satisfaction beyond this life is not only true of rock stars it is also true of professional athletes. It is true of all of us.

Look for instance at the tragic deaths of Len Bias and Don Rogers, who in 1986 both died just days apart from each other. They both overdosed on cocaine. Len Bias was the second overall NBA draft pick but died before he could play a single professional game. Don Rogers was an NFL player and recognized as an "All-American," yet his career and life were cut short. We could also look at Dwight Gooden and his sordid decline.

---

[15] Ibid., 217-18.

BROKEN CISTERNS OR ABOUNDING STREAM?

Typically, people would think these men had everything; surely, they would be happy. Yet, even they were seeking. Seeking for satisfaction that can't ultimately be met here. God has given humanity amazing hardware and bandwidth for joy but too often we download stuff we're not compatible with and so we're left buffering until our whole system crashes.

Humanity has a hole, a longing, a search for more.[16] Humanity is drinking from a broken cistern.

Enter *sehnsucht*. *Sehnsucht* is a German term that communicates the longing that all of humanity has. It means "longing," "yearning," or "craving." It is a way of saying "something is intensely missing, there must be more." *Sehnsucht* is related to worship because worship has to do with estimation of good and our pursuit and enjoyment of it. Thus the longing that we all have is a type of worship. We *all* worship. It's not just something we do. It's who we are. We are all worshipers.

When we seek for other things to fill us, make us whole, fill our void, it doesn't work. Those other things merely work their ruin.

---

[16] Humanities search though often unrealized is a search for the Divine. Calvin said "a sense of Deity is inscribed on every heart" (*Institutes*, 1.3.1). People often suppress their desire for God, their ultimate good, and seek to find meaning and life in subordinate goods or things which are sheared of all good.

BROKEN CISTERNS OR ABOUNDING STREAM?

When we, like our first parents, turn from God to listen to, and find our life ultimately in others things, it damns us. Romans says that when we know God but don't honor Him as God then we become futile in our thinking, and our foolish hearts become darkened. We may claim to be wise, but we're fools. Because we exchange the glory of the immortal God for other things, foolish things, like sex, success, and a sordid amount of other things.

This type of wickedness leads to more wickedness because we're left to our foolish lusty
hearts. This all happens because we exchange the truth about God for a lie and worship and serve the creature and all our vain desires instead of the Creator, who is blessed forever! How foolish we are (cf. Rom. 1:21-26)! And how terrible the consequences for our foolish sin...

In John 4 Jesus confronted a woman who was also desperately looking for more, and looking in the wrong places. She essentially exchanged the glory and worship of God for a lie, for something else.

This woman at the well, this woman is very much like you and me, she had five previous husbands and the guy she was then with was just a boyfriend or maybe "partner" or "special friend." This lady, like many drug addicts, was on the fringes of society. The Samaritan woman may not have had a substance abuse problem but she has the same problem any addict has, any sinner has, a heart problem.

She was drinking deeply of stagnate waters. She knew of the restless heart that Augustine spoke of, she knew of the God-shaped vacuum, because such was her heart. She was addicted to, yea worshiping, something other than the LORD God, even though she tried to cover it in her religious garb.

ABOUNDING STREAMS

So what does the soul physician offer her as a cure? This woman had been drinking in so much, and searching so much, but her thirst was never quenched. Jesus offers her living water, He offers her Himself. He offers her meaningful worship through the Spirit, that is to say, communion with God.[17]

Jesus has even given us a foretaste of the new creation and the relationship with Him that we all long for. He has given us His Spirit

---

[17] Cf. relevant verses Gen. 2:8-10; 26:19; Ps. 42:1-2; Is. 12:3; 33:21; 44:3; 55:1-3; Jer. 17:13; Zech. 14:8; Ezek. 47:1-12; Songs. 4:15; Ps. 36:9; John 4:10-11; 6:35; 7:37-39; Rev. 7:17; 22:1. Although, not directly, all these verses refer back to fellowship with God being restored. This is what we all truly long for though we seek for it in other things, other idols. We long for Eden, we long for restored fellowship with God. May we say with the psalmist, "As a deer pants for flowing streams, so pants my soul for you, O God. My soul thirsts for God, for the living God. When shall I come and appear before God?" (Ps. 42:1-2).

as a "down payment" on what is to come. He is already working on renewing all things and He is already giving us amazing joy. He has given us the Comforter that cries out that we are sons and daughters of God. Jesus is taking our sinful and broken heart and renewing it. He is taking our old busted heart of stone and giving us a heart of flesh that beats for Him with new invigorating life.

Truly, Jesus alone "satisfies the longing soul, and the hungry soul He fills with good things" (Ps. 107:9 cf. Ps. 42:1-2). Jesus is the way, the truth, and the life (Jn. 14:6 cf. 1 Tim. 2:5). He alone gives people new birth (Jn. 3; Eph. 2:1-6), new identities (Rom. 6:20-22; Eph. 2:1-10; Col. 2:13; 3:7-17), and a completely new heart that is empowered to do His will (Jer. 24:7; Ezek. 36:26-27), free from enslaving sin (Rom. 6:20-22; 7:15-25).[18] In Jesus our longing soul finds satisfaction. In Jesus we have, even now, eternal life (Jn. 17:3). Christ gives the shalom that the world can never give (Jn. 14:27).

Oh, don't content yourself with anything less than fullness of joy and pleasures forevermore, anything less than God in the face

---

[18] Powlison points out that "when the analysis of what is wrong does not lead directly to our need for the person and work of the Messiah, then that analysis is shallow. The solution necessarily becomes some version of 'Peace, peace,' when there is no peace" (David Powlison, *Seeing with New Eyes: Counseling and the Human Condition through the Lens of Scripture* [Phillipsburg, NJ: P&R Publishing, 2003], 238).

of Jesus Christ. Don't settle for anything else, spend and be spent for God and His glory.

SLAVE (A POEM)

Addiction, the affliction we embrace.
Drowning in more,
yet never full,
we consume the poison.

Freedom from the substance,
freedom from the porn,
is what we yearn,
yet ever embrace our shackles.

Numbing ecstasy,
this misery.

Bound by this high,
damaged by this drink.

Party
or prison,
this prism through which we peer.

Addiction,
this affliction,
for which we ever yearn.

We burn,
burn out,
and repeat the syndrome.

BROKEN CISTERNS OR ABOUNDING STREAM?

No end in sight,
all is night,
an endless cycle down.

Yes, dirt and sand
is all this land,
as we thirst for peace and joy.

An empty well
is where we dwell,
no thirst is quenched
below.

But as I gaze
upon Your grave,
where for me You bled,
my shackles break
and to You take
rest from all this hell.

Slave to sin,
never again;
You my Master alone.

Yet why do I embrace this noose that holds me?

Lord, why do I run to a whore
when I know all she has in store for me
is death?

BROKEN CISTERNS OR ABOUNDING STREAM?

I see the light,
the joy,
and close my eyes,
and turn away.

Why don't I stay?

I run to the slaughter
but You've prepared a feast.

I slit my wrist,
when for me You bled.

O' the misery
that is me,
when I turn away.

Why don't I stay?

You quench my thirst,
all else is empty wells.

Why swallow up this gravel,
when You have abounding streams?

O' the misery that is me, apart from You.

TAKE AWAY

- Do you realize that your sin, whatever it is, is a broken cistern? It can't fulfill.

BROKEN CISTERNS OR ABOUNDING STREAM?

It can't quench your thirst. Pray that God would help you remember this even in the midst of your battle against temptation.
- Where are you placing your hope and trust? Where are you seeking fulfillment? Money? Friends? Success? Substances? Relationships? Being good? All those things will fall short.
- Do you realize only God can quench your thirst? Read, pray, meditate on Psalm 16:11.
- Pursue a relationship with God. Pray that it would be dynamic and life giving but realize it will not always be "fireworks." There will be days when you "don't feel it" but God is still God and His truth is still truth. And soon we shall see Him face to face (Matt. 5:8; 1 Jn. 3:2). All our longings will be met!
- Think about the vicious cycle of sin. Think about your desire. Yet, think how it never *truly* fulfills. Our desire is broken. This world is broken. What this tells us is that we have a desire within us that this world cannot fulfill. We long for a *new* earth in which righteousness dwells (2 Peter 3:13).

5
IT IS A HEART PROBLEM

Jesus tells us that "the good person out of the good treasure of his heart produces good, and the evil person out of his evil treasure produces evil, for out of the abundance of the heart his mouth speaks" (Lk. 6:45 cf. Matt. 12:35; 15:18-19). Jesus is saying that whatever comes out of us—substance abuse, lust, gluttony, or pride—flows from our hearts. The external issues that are visible, whatever they are, are signs of an inner festering and decimating problem that flows outward as a sign of the inner disease.

IT IS A HEART PROBLEM

The Bible's approach to enslaving sin is essential because unlike others programs19 it gets to the root of the problem, the heart. Some may object that Alcoholics Anonymous and other programs do get at the heart issues;20 however, Jesus alone "satisfies the longing soul, and the hungry soul He fills with good things" (Ps. 107:9 cf. Ps. 42:1-2). Jesus is the way, the truth, and the life (Jn. 14:6 cf. 1 Tim. 2:5). He alone gives people new birth (Jn. 3; Eph. 2:1-6), new identities (Rom. 6:20-22; Eph. 2:1-10; Col. 2:13; 3:7-17), and a completely new heart that is empowered to do His will (Jer. 24:7; Ezek. 36:26-27), free

---

[19] Secular people, even trained secular people, and support groups cannot sufficiently guide and encourage people spiritually. Why? Because they are spiritually discerned (1 Cor. 2:14). Further, they will point you to the wrong solutions, though, that is not to say that we cannot learn from them. We certainly can, and must. Unbelievers very often exceed Christians educationally and intellectually but they do not have the enlightening presence of the Holy Spirit.

[20] I am not against involvement in all non-Christian programs. Yet, non-Christian programs cannot get to what is at the heart of the problem. There is a necessary shallowness to all other programs. All other programs are also limited to the amount of correct solutions that they can come to because they are founded on faulty worldviews. All of this is not to say that all Christian programs are better. That is not true. However, I would say they have the *potential* to be better and should be better. Again, what is truly needed is life change that comes from heart change (Rom. 6:17; 2 Cor. 5:17; Gal. 5:22–23; Phil. 2:12; Heb. 8:10). It will not be helpful in the long run if one goes from drunkenness to a sober self-righteous formality (John Owen, *Overcoming Sin and Temptation,* 85). Actually, defeating sin from self-strength with self-righteousness goals is the soul and substance of all false religion in the world (Ibid., 47).

IT IS A HEART PROBLEM

from the enslaving sin of addiction (Rom. 6:20-22; 7:15-25).[21]

We can deal with externals all day but we really need to get to the issues from which they flow. We can smash bees all day, and we do at my house, but what we really need to do is destroy the nest from which they all come (see Ps. 36:1; Matt. 12:35; 15:18-20; Lk. 6:45; Prov. 4:23). We do not just want behavioral modification, that is too shallow. We do not want our counselee to drink less from broken cisterns or from different broken cisterns, we want to lead them to drink from the well of living water. Our aim is not mere modification but transformation, and this truly comes from the inside out.

Timothy Keller has helpfully said,

> *Moralistic behavior change* bends *a person into a different pattern through fear of consequences rather than* melting *a person into a new shape. But this does not work. If you try to bend a piece of metal without the softening effect of heat, it is likely to snap back to its former position. This is why we see*

---

[21] Powlison points out that "when the analysis of what is wrong does not lead directly to our need for the person and work of the Messiah, then that analysis is shallow. The solution necessarily becomes some version of 'Peace, peace,' when there is no peace" (*Seeing with New Eyes*, 238).

IT IS A HEART PROBLEM

> *people try to change through moralistic behaviorism find themselves repeatedly lapsing into sin... But the gospel of God's grace doesn't try to bend a heart into a new pattern; it melts it and re-forms it into a new shape. The gospel can produce a new joy, love, and gratitude—new inclinations of the heart that eat away at deadly self-regard and self-concentration.[22]*

We need to get to the root of the problem. Think of it this way, if a toilet is clogged and continually spewing forth all sorts of filth what is the immediate thing to do? Should we automatically grab a mop and try to keep up cleaning the floor as the toilet continues to overflow? Or should we take a different approach to the situation, should we get down to the *heart* of the problem and kill the source of the mess?

We should not take a mop to the problems of society. We must seek to change the heart of the problem, sinful hearts, by the gospel of Christ. The gospel alone is the power to salvation, sanctification, and thus societal change; even the changing of substance abusers and porn addicts.

---

[22] Timothy Keller, *Center Church* (Grand Rapids: Zondervan, 2012), 67.

IT IS A HEART PROBLEM

What needs to happen is the addict needs to stop trusting and worshiping the pleasure, comfort, coping ability, and all the other supposed benefits of the substance and turn to the LORD God. That is the problem. But how is it addressed? If the person is a Christian is the problem automatically fixed? Or if they start having a really good time at Sunday morning worship will their temptation to heroin leave altogether? Not likely. We need to have a holistic approach to help the person struggling with the enslaving sin. Obviously, the main problem is the main problem, and that must be dealt with, and that is the heart problem. However, to truly help, and to help as Jesus did, is to minster to the whole person. Depending on the enslaving sin that is being dealt with, this may involve social issues, physical issues, financial issues, and so forth.[23]

---

[23] Jesus had a holistic approach to ministry. He ministered in word and deed. He cared about people's spiritual, physical, and social condition. Jesus would heal people (often physically and spiritually) and thus they could enter back into society (cf. Mk. 1:40-45). We should also seek to have a holistic ministry. We must remember, however, that Jesus Christ is people's biggest need. The gravest need that people have is not to be made right physically or even reconciled socially, but reconciled, made right, before a holy and just God. People's biggest need is that they be reconciled to God; not government, not family, not society, God. There is only one way for this to possibly happen: The gospel of Jesus Christ. We should deeply care about people and seek to serve them but through all we do we must seek to point to Jesus who served us through the cross to reconcile us to God.

IT IS A HEART PROBLEM

I have talked to many addicts that live in very hostile situations for anyone but particularly for an addict. If something goes wrong in their atmosphere they know how to handle it. They know just what to go to, old trusty is there for them. Through the good and the bad. If life is bad, medicate. If it is going good, make it better, medicate. Whatever this "medicating" is, it has formed a truly deadly habit.

William Moyers basically said, in his autobiography *Broken: My Story of Addiction and Redemption*, that most people take painkillers for pain but that he took marijuana when his heart ached. It didn't fix the pain for very long though.[24]

Yet getting high was what Moyers lived for. When he didn't feel good he knew what he could do to fix it, get high. And that's what he did. Drugs were his strong tower, his refuge, his hiding place. The very words that the psalmist very often uses to describe the LORD God (cf. Ps. 5:11; 32:7; 61:3; 119:114).

As Christians, the LORD is to be our strong tower, the one we run to when things are bad (and good). We all struggle to trust as we should but the addict especially runs from the LORD to their substance or porn. However,

---

[24] William Cope Moyers with Katherine Ketchham, *Broken: My Story of Addiction and Redemption* (New York: Viking, 2006), 44.

IT IS A HEART PROBLEM

their "strong tower" is really a cage. It enslaves them.

THE PROBLEM IS NOT SIMPLISTIC

Though addiction, heroin, alcohol, or otherwise, at its root is a heart problem, there is still other components to consider. We should not have a simplistic approach to these problems. We should not think that one size fits all. We cannot expect to say the same couple of verses to each addict and tell them to repent and go on our way and think we are done with helping them. That would not be helpful, or biblical. Instead, as we have pointed out, counsel must be appropriately nuanced (cf. Acts 20:35; Rom. 15:1; 1 Cor. 15:1; 1 Thess. 5:14; 2 Tim. 4:2).

We need to address the heart because what enters our hearts will eventually flow out of our hearts but where is the heart situated? It is vitally connected to the body. We are psychosomatic unities—body and heart/soul.[25] So as we address the heart/soul we must not forget the physical component.

---

[25] Martyn Lloyd-Jones knew that, "You cannot isolate the spiritual from the physical" (*Spiritual Depression* [Grand Rapids: Wm. B. Eerdmans Publishing Company, 1968], 9). Early on Jonathan Edwards realized this. He said, "Such seems to be our nature, and such the laws of soul and body, that there never is any case whatsoever, any lively and vigorous exercise of the inclination, without some effect upon the body" (Jonathan Edwards, "A Treatise Concerning Religious Affections," 237 in *The Works of Jonathan Edwards,* vol. 1, [Carlisle, PA: The Banner of Truth Trust, 2009]).

IT IS A HEART PROBLEM

We must also not forget the cognitive, emotive, and volition side of our souls (see figure 1.3 above). Our approach should always be biblical but to be biblical is always to be nuanced and sensitive to the particular circumstance that we are addressing (1 Thess. 5:14).

For example, as we minister to heroin addicts we must remember that God created us as body-soul beings. Addicts "kicking" heroin undergo physical withdrawal symptoms that are difficult. We must take seriously the influence that physical difficulties have on people. We must analyze the people we are seeking to help and remember that we are all at the same saints, sufferers, and sinners.[26]

TAKE AWAY

- Do you understand the importance of getting to the root of the problem? We could spray and squash bees all day but unless we get to the queen we're going to continue to have all sorts of problems.
- Are you just squashing bees or are you trying to get to the root of the problem? When battling your

---

[26] See Michael R. Emlet's book *CrossTalk: Where Life and Scripture Meet* (Greensboro, NC: New Growth Press, 2009), 93-106.

IT IS A HEART PROBLEM

addiction don't deviate all your attention to peripheral issues. Realize you work at getting to the fundamental issues.

- Have you ever been guilty of over-simplifying the problem of addiction? Do you think there's a quick fix? A pill, rehab, or counseling? There is no quick fix. And simply saying, "Stop it, stop it, stop it," will not work.
- Do you see your addiction as a dynamic problem or do naïvely think there is a quick fix? There are answers and helps but there is no "silver bullet."

PART TWO: THE TRANSFORMATION PROCESS

"Sanctify them in the truth, Your word is truth."
– John 17:17

"Abide in me, and I in you. As the branch cannot bear fruit by itself, unless it abides in the vine, neither can you, unless you abide in me... I am the vine; you are the branches. Whoever abides in me and I in him, he it is that bears much fruit, for apart from me you can do nothing... These things I have spoken to you, that my joy may be in you, and that your joy may be full."
– John 15:4-5, 11

"Do not be conformed to this world, but be transformed by the renewal of your mind."
– Romans 12:2

"Do not get drunk with wine,... but be filled with the Spirit, addressing one another in psalms and hymns and spiritual songs, singing and making melody to the Lord with your heart."
– Ephesians 5:18-19

6
WHAT FORMS AND (RE)FORMS YOU?

INTRODUCTION

We're shaped by a whole host of things—constitution, genetics, socioeconomic factors, health, education, culture, upbringing, etc.; and we are (re)shaped by a few, consciously and subconsciously. Therefore, we see the importance of understanding how it is that we are transformed. For when we know how transformation takes place we can make a better conscious effort at transformation.

We're shaped by one of two gods, one of two voices. The god of this world (Jn. 12:31; Eph. 2:2-3; 6:12), or the one true God. There are two masters with two different sets of commands, we will obey one of them (Matt.

6:24; Lk. 16:13). We will be slaves—that's inevitable (Rom. 6). The question is: *To whom*?

And with what result? Life or death (Rom. 6:23)? We're shaped by one of two kingdoms. Our kingdom, informed by Satan; or, God's Kingdom, informed by God.

This section is not concerned with which kingdom we *should* desire. It is assumed that we should desire the Kingdom of God. This chapter is concerned with helping us understand how we are (re)shaped or transformed to desire the right Kingdom. This is a more difficult task than it would first appear. However, if you know Scripture, and indeed your own heart, you know this is a difficult task. Yet, it is terribly grave and important (e.g. think of Judas desiring his own kingdom and thus betraying the Messiah and the *true* Kingdom).

We *are* being shaped. But how? And by what?

A BRIEF STORY

Jesus transforms and brings life, even when the metamorphosis process is painful. Isaac's testimony demonstrates this.

Isaac was a cocaine addict that ignored his mother's repeated words: "God's going to change you, it's going to hurt, but He's going to change you."

WHAT FORMS AND (RE)FORMS YOU?

One day Isaac was abducted and tortured. He was punched in his stomach until he couldn't breath. Then he was blindfolded and punched repeatedly. He was stripped to his underwear and put in a shower where he was shocked repeatedly. Eventually they put belts around his body so he couldn't move. They forced him into a bathtub and filled up the water so that his whole body was submerged except his mouth and nose. Then they began to shock him again.

The pain was unbearable.

That's when his mother's words came true. God changed Isaac. Isaac turned to Jesus. He was at his end. So he turned to Jesus. And Jesus saved him, spiritually and physically.

A different guy walked in the room and told the men to let him go. And they did. Isaac lived. And he was given new life. Eternal life. He was transformed. But the transformation did not work itself out automatically.

So, how was Isaac transformed in his day-to-day life?

DEFINITIONS

Putting things in categories, like putting things in containers, is helpful. However, their strength lies where their fault lies: they keep things that naturally run together from running together. With food this is helpful for taste, with thoughts it is helpful for understanding, but, when it's all said and done, we must realize that containers like categories do not finally keep the contents apart. They are helpful, and perhaps necessary, but in the end affect (and yet assist) precision. Our categories are: 1) knowledge, 2) worship, and 3) practice. Below is a figure that shows their interconnected relationship (Figure 1).

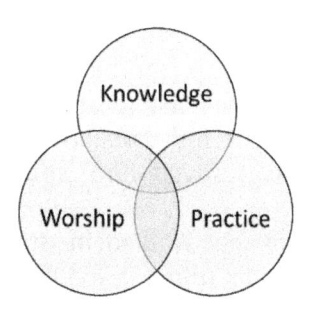

Figure 1. The Interconnectedness of Knowledge, Worship, and Practice in Transformation.

Knowledge

By "knowledge" I mean worldview or view of our chief end or "the good." Worldview deals with more then what we see as "the good." However, it does, or should, also shape what we see as our ultimate goal as well. A worldview answers questions and tells the story of our existence, but it must also tell us where, if anywhere, that story is going or should go.

Notice also that it's not just the intentional thinker or the Christian that is shaped by a worldview, by knowledge. We are *all* shaped and informed by what we know, or think we know. For instance, the sex addict and gangster are shaped by a worldview, even if it is a sub-conscious and unarticulated form of hedonism or nihilism. However, I do believe that one will be shaped more when one's knowledge or worldview is more explicit. So, perhaps a sex addict who is also a convinced and proud naturalistic hedonist will have less restraint when it comes to illegal sexual practices (e.g. rape, prostitution, etc.); rather, for him it is more a practical matter of will he be caught, than a question of whether such and such practice is ethical or not.[27]

Worship

What then is "worship"? Worship here is the (often purposeful and artistic) ingesting of "the good." This definition equally applies to the sex addict watching porn, the gangster listening to rap, and the Christian singing

---

[27] Our worldviews have consequences, good or bad. R.C. Sproul shows this in his book *The Consequences of Ideas.* Friedrich Nietzsche even said in *Beyond Good and Evil* that philosophy always creates a world in it's own image, it cannot do anything different.

songs, meditating on Scripture, or celebrating the Lord's Supper. Worship, as you can see, very clearly incorporates both the two other categories. Worship is, you could say, the conscious (and also subconscious) practice (our second category) of thinking about something (our first category).

Practice

Practice is the conscious and subconscious practices that shape our life. What some have explained as thick and thin habits or practices.[28] These habitual practices have greater or lesser effects upon us depending upon their significance.

What we do has effects upon who we are and what we will be. So, for example, when three different types of men see an attractive lady jogging on the side of the road they will have three different responses because of their conscious and subconscious practices that are ingrained in them through their "knowledge" and "worship." Yet, their practices, as we'll see, serve to further their worship and knowledge.

So, for example, the sex addict will undress the attractive jogger. This will in part be because of his worship and knowledge and will yet undergird and inform his worship

---

[28] See James K. A. Smith's insightful book *Desiring the Kingdom: Worship, Worldview, and Cultural Formation* (Grand Rapids, Baker Academic, 2009), esp. 80-85.

and knowledge. He will in a sense say to himself subconsciously that his knowledge of things is justified by the image of this woman and his worship is also justified. The gangster will have a similar response. But, perhaps to a different end; he may think of all the money he could make with her body. The Christian man also informed by his knowledge and worship will pray for the jogger; or, perhaps, not look at her so as not to be tempted.

Whatever the specific example, we see that our knowledge, worship, and practices have a very real impact on us and how we are shaped. Each aspect serves it's purpose, yet it is closely tied to the other two. We cannot neglect any aspect or the fact that they are closely interconnected. Now that we have defined each category, we will look at each aspect in more detail.

HOW ARE WE TRANSFORMED?

In Aristotle's terms our view of "the good" is reshaped by knowledge.[29] And, in catechismal terms, if our chief end is to glorify God and enjoy Him forever[30] it will necessarily have a specific impact on our lives. That is just the way we are as humans. We all, without

---

[29] *Aristotle's Nicomachean Ethics* Trans. Robert C. Bartlett and Susan D. Collins (The University of Chicago Press: Chicago, 2011), 4 (1095a14), cf. 309.

[30] From the first question of the Westminster Shorter Catechism.

exception, live towards our chief end, our view of the "good life." However, this is messy, there are many things and ideas which vie for this place. Thus the importance of knowledge rightly directed (i.e. wisdom), worship, and habits; all of which inform, play off, and undergird the others (see Figure 2 below). Notice also that it is not just the Christian that worships, all men do (e.g. the gangster has a certain type of rap music that glorifies his view of the good life).

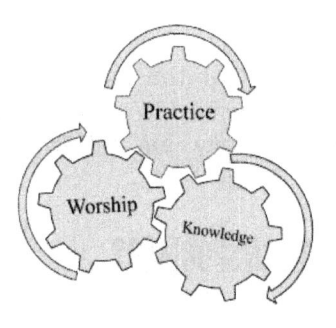

Figure 2. The Reciprocal Transforming Relationship of Knowledge, Worship, and Practice.

It is clear then that right and good worship is vital because it exalts and holds

WHAT FORMS AND (RE)FORMS YOU?

before us our chief end. If our worship has as its object the wrong thing we will thus go wrong in innumerable ways (cf. Rom. 1:18-32). Because of this, the reformation of our lives is a slow, and often painful, process. Witness the fall (the body of the book) and rise (the epilogue) of Raskolnikov from Dostoyevsky's *Crime and Punishment.* If we dig ourselves into a ditch we do not magically rise out of it (cf. Prov. 26:27). We have to dig ourselves out of it. Of course, as Christians we do believe that the Spirit assists us (e.g. Jn. 14:16). Yet, the fact remains, transformation is difficult and does not finally occur here.

Scripture and reality are not at odds. We are shaped by what we know, worship, and do (and these are all interrelated). Scripture tells us to know the LORD, worship Him, and serve Him and thus be transformed. We see this same type of thing when we understand the relationship of faith and works, and the relationship of indicative and imperative. We know/believe God's truth (faith), therefore we worship, and have corresponding actions (works). Again, when we (rightly and supernaturally) understand God's truth (indicative) we will worship, which in turn will change the way we live (imperative).

In Scripture we see huge importance placed on listening to He who speaks wisdom, the LORD, and not to the father of lies, Satan. We see this especially in the beginning. Eve

WHAT FORMS AND (RE)FORMS YOU?

listens to the serpent's words and disregards the LORD's, and chaos and curse ensue. However, notice that she did not just receive information/knowledge or believe the wrong source. Her desires were also wrongly informed. Because Eve listened to the serpent she saw the tree as delightful. She saw the tree as desirable (Gen. 3:6). Thus she fell.

As the Scripture says, "Each person is tempted when he is lured and enticed by his own *desire*. Then desire when it has conceived gives birth to sin, and sin when it is fully grown brings forth death" (James 1:14-15). We, thus, resist the devil by being firm in the faith. We, like Jesus, fight off wicked desires with God's Word. Satan would have us be reconstituted by his words, wicked untruth, yet we combat his lies by teaching ourselves to desire good things by the implantation of God's words, the truth (e.g. the place of Prov. 7:1-5 in the larger context of Prov. 7). When we feed on the Word of God the metabolic result is a healthy representation of God. God would have us (re)shaped into His image, the image of His Son. Conversely, Satan would have us formed into what C.S. Lewis called the "unman."

Our thinking and our beliefs play a large part but we are tempted not by thinking and believing but by our desires (recall James 1:14-15 from above). I do think, however, that thinking and beliefs are the atmosphere in

WHAT FORMS AND (RE)FORMS YOU?

which desire lives. They are the soil and habitat; they're the ocean in which desire can swim. Thinking and believing are not unimportant. Eve would have never sinned had she not heard Satan's "knowledge" and believed him. Yet, we are understanding Eve, and ourselves, wrongly, if we don't also realize that she desired (again, recall Gen. 3:6; also Eph. 2:3 says that we also once carried out the *desires* of the flesh).

I think it also must be noted here that our desires are shaped by our thinking and believing but they are also shaped by less conscious things. I am quite sure, for instance, that quite a few Nazi Youth did not read Hitler's *Mein Kampf* but yet were shaped by the very same image. This was because they lived and breathed and ingested it's teaching, though not mainly consciously, but because it was the cultural air they breathed.

We have a lot of things externally and internally that seek to shape us. As Calvin has famously said, we are idol factories. That's why we see much emphasis in Scripture placed on loving God with our *whole* heart (cf. e.g. 1 Chron. 12:38; 28:9; 29:9, 19; 2 Chron. 15:15; 16:9; 19:9; 25:2; Ps. 9:1; 16:9; 86:12), not just a portion of it.

We temper our hearts variously through understanding (cf. Deut. 6:4-9; 1 Kings 18:21; Neh. 8), worship (e.g. Ps.; Eph. 5:18-20) and practice (e.g. Rom. 12:1; Col. 3:2). That's how

WHAT FORMS AND (RE)FORMS YOU?

we're shaped biblically and practically. The more we have our chief end in view and the better our chief end is the better we will live.

For instance, Jesus reasons with us in Matthew 6:19-24 about desire. He shows that what is in our best interest, i.e. what we *should* desire, is laying up treasure in heaven. He tells us specifically in verse 21 that what we desire, i.e. "treasure," will bring the rest of us along (i.e. "heart"). So, again, Eve was led into sin because she desired ("treasured") the fruit. Our battle is thus the battle of treasuring, desiring. That's why sex education doesn't work, for example. You can show a bunch of kids images of a bunch of nasty things and tell them a bunch of bad stories. But, in the end, if sex is what they treasure then that's what they'll do. After all, that is what is glorified on the screen and in our culture.

On the positive side, Paul lived the way he did, and died the way he did, not merely because of his cognitive understanding or because of his beliefs; but because of what he *desired* (though, as we have said, they are closely related). Paul, in his letter to the Philippians, tells us of the desire that fueled his powerful life. He drove on through thick and thin because he had counted everything as loss because of the surpassing worth of knowing Christ Jesus his Lord. For Christ's sake Paul suffered the loss of all things and counted them as rubbish, in order that he may gain Christ (Phil. 3:8).

Truly, wherever our treasure (i.e. desire, view of "the good," or our view of the good life) is, our heart ("heart" in Scripture has to do with our whole self; cognition, volition, emotions) will be also (Matt. 6:21; Lk. 12:34).

How's Isaac Doing Today?

Isaac remembers how lifeless his previous life was. He works at treasuring the gospel of Jesus above everything. He knows that if he fails to treasure the gospel as he should he could fall into sin again like he has seen others do.

Isaac fights against sin by increasing his knowledge of God. He's reading theology. He has made a practice of discipling the young men around him. Isaac also teaches himself to worship the Lord by proclaiming the gospel in song. He did not previously sing but God placed a new song in his heart and now he leads worship at an orphanage where he ministers and works.

TAKE AWAY

- Do you realize the importance of understanding the shaping influences in your life?
- If we are transformed by knowledge, worship, and practices, how do you

WHAT FORMS AND (RE)FORMS YOU?

think they can transform us? How should our everyday life be different? In biblical language, what practices should you strive to "put on" and what should you strive to "put off" (see e.g. Col. 3:1-17)?

- What negative sinful influences are shaping you? Think of the music you listen to, what you think about, watch, etc.
- What positive God-honoring influences are shaping you? Think of the gathering on Sunday with the church, the church community, what you read, what you sing, etc.

7
BE MINDFUL OF YOUR MIND

INTRODUCTION
What is the place of the mind in our fight against enslaving sin? Is thinking relevant to the fight? What, if any, emphasis should we place on the importance of knowledge? Does hard thinking bring any beneficial fruit or is the tree bare, shorn of any value?

If we boil down and distill Christianity, the remaining content is not logical argument. Christianity is more than a philosophy, more than a religion. It is more than cognitive assent. It is more than a social club. Christianity is not simply about ritual. It is not just about emotions. It is not just about the mind.

BE MINDFUL OF YOUR MIND

Christianity is a relationship with a God who has made Himself known. It is more than formulas and repetition of rote words; though there are meaningful words and ceremonies. Christianity is something that must be believed, but belief is merely the beginning (though it must continue). Christianity gives true—chasm bridging—fellowship, but is not merely a fellowship. Christianity *is* a philosophy, indeed, *the* philosophy. We, in a sense, worship wisdom incarnate.[31] But still, Christianity is not just a philosophy.

Christianity is not just about thinking and knowing. Yet, thinking and knowing are vital.

The Christian mind is vital because it is emphatic in Scripture.[32] It is vital because it is vital in our fight of faith. It is vital because we are commanded to worship the LORD with all we are, our mind included (Matt. 22:37; Mk. 12:30; Lk. 10:27).

The Christian mind *is* very important. Yet, where do we see this in Scripture? Why is this the case? And what affect does it have?

---

[31] The Word (*Logos*) became flesh and dwelt among us, and we have seen His glory (Jn. 1:14). In Jesus are hidden all the treasures of wisdom and knowledge (Col. 2:3).

[32] Cf. Ps. 9:10; 32:8-9; 73:22; 119:34; Prov. 2:1-6; Is. 1:18; Matt. 13:19; 22:37; Mk. 12:30; Lk. 10:27; Jn. 8:32; 13:17; Acts 17:2-4; 20:28; Rom. 6:17; 8:5-6; 10:13-14, 17; 12:2; 1 Cor. 2:6, 14-16; 3:1-2; 14:13-15, 20; 2 Cor. 4:3-6; 5:11; Eph. 1:17-19; 3:14-19; 4:23; Phil. 1:9-11; 4:8-9; Col. 1:9-10, 28; 3:1-2, 10; Heb. 5:11-6:3; 2 Pet. 1:5.

BE MINDFUL OF YOUR MIND
THE CHRISTIAN MIND AND THE BIBLE

The Bible shows us that the Christian mind is very important.[33] Thinking for Christians is not just theoretical, it is practical. We trust God because we *know* Him (Ps. 9:10).

God tells us to think. He tells us He will teach us, yet we must learn and not be like animals without understanding (Ps. 32:8-9 cf. 73:22). In fact, we must learn so that we can obey (Josh. 1:8-9; Ps. 37:31; 86:11; 95:10; 119:11, 34).

We are told in multiple passages to relentlessly pursue knowledge/wisdom (e.g. Prov. 2:1-6). We are to seek it as silver and gold. For it is worth more than silver or gold (Job 28:15-19; Ps. 119:72, 127; Prov. 3:14; 8:10, 19).

The Apostle Paul is a prime example of the importance of the mind in the Christian life.[34] He instructs us to take every thought as a prisoner, to capture them and make them obey Christ our Master (cf. 2 Cor. 10:5). Knowledge and thoughts are not wrong. They are good when rightly directed. That is, to Christ and His glory (cf. 1 Cor. 10:31).

---

[33] That is partly why it's vital that Christian leaders know the truth, are able to teach it, and defend it (cf. 1 Tim. 3:2; 4:13; 2 Tim. 2:15, 24; Titus 1:9).

[34] Paul himself had an amazing intellect. He thoroughly knew Scripture but he also knew and incorporated other writings (cf. Acts 17:28; Titus 1:12).

BE MINDFUL OF YOUR MIND

It was Paul's custom to *reason* from the Scriptures and prove that Jesus was the Christ (Acts 17:2-4).[35] This was not purely academic —it lead to worship or rejection, new life or death—but it was academic. Paul also repeatedly told his disciples to set their minds on God's truth (cf. Rom. 8:5-6; Phil. 4:8-9; Col. 3:1-2) and not on evil things. In Paul's letters to the Corinthians we often see the refrain "do you not *know*" (1 Cor. 3:16; 5:6; 6:2-3, 9, 15-16, 19; also Rom. 6:3, 16). In fact, Paul tells us that we cannot be saved apart from some form of knowledge (Rom. 10:13-14, 17). Yet, knowledge is not just essential in salvation but also in sanctification. We are transformed, in part, through knowledge (e.g. Rom. 12:2; Col. 3:10).[36] That is why many of Paul's prayers have as their goal the increase of knowledge (Eph. 1:17-19; 3:14-19; Phil. 1:9-11; Col. 1:9-10).

We are to have a zeal for God, but it is supposed to be according to knowledge (Rom. 10:2). God rewards those who seek Him (Heb. 11:6), and our seeking of God is, at least in part, through knowledge. Yes, we worship

---

[35] Paul is not the only one that used reason. John wrote a book that we would believe that Jesus is the Messiah (Jn. 20:31). Luke also gave an orderly account so that we may have certainty concerning the things that have been taught about Messiah Jesus (Lk. 1:1-4).

[36] Paul says that he proclaims Messiah and teaches *so that* he may present everyone mature in Christ (Col. 1:28). Thus our maturity, our (trans)formation, comes partly through knowledge.

God with our spirit through the Spirit—amen! —yet, we use our minds also (1 Cor. 14:15).[37]

The role of the mind in the Bible is a life-supporting organ. Apart from it the Christian would have no life; or, if he did, it would be small, sad, and stunted (1 Cor. 14:20; Heb. 5:11-6:3). Therefore, we must pursue knowledge/wisdom and we must pray for it. Our hands, head, and knees, so to speak, must be weary in pursuit.[38]

We must set our mind on things above, where Christ is, not on the temptations of the earth (see Col. 3:1ff).

THE CHRISTIAN MIND AND WORSHIP

The Christian mind is important because it informs our worship; which in turn informs everything we do. Including, or especially, our fight against sin.

First, and fundamental to everything we do and are, is worship. It informs everything; even our reading of this, what we think of knowledge, and all things in general. We are first and foremost, not thinking or believing

---

[37] Notice that even a Pentecost Peter was using his mind to exegete Scripture. Peter used scriptural proofs and not some vain senseless banter to make his (inspired) point (Acts. 2:14-41).

[38] Of course, we must remember, understanding comes through dual illumination (2 Tim. 2:7). We think over God's truth and He gives us understanding. It is our work and it is the Spirit's work.

BE MINDFUL OF YOUR MIND

beings,[39] but worshipers. We desire; we love. Everything else gets pulled along. Yet, it is knowledge, our minds, which can shape our desires. So that, in part, is why we are exhorted to meditate on God's truth (cf. Josh. 1:8; Ps. 77:12; 119:15; 143:5; Jn. 17:17). God's truth is life changing, in part, because it changes us, mainly though changing what we desire, what we see as "the good life."[40]

Thus it is difficult to speak on this subject with scientific precision. All these categories —worship, practice, and knowledge—are interrelated; they have a cyclical and reciprocal relationship. They affirm and build upon the other. We tend to think on what we worship and we have habits shaped by what we worship and think on. Then, our habits undergird and support our thinking and worship yet again. And on it goes.[41] This, depending on what we worship, is a vicious or a precious cycle.

---

[39] See Smith, *Desiring the Kingdom*.

[40] So, for example, Jn. 14:14 is true not because of some magical incantation but because God changes our desires. When we begin to see that in God's presence there is fullness of joy our vision of the "good life" is recast and thus are strivings go in a different direction. Instead of seeking our kingdom, our name, we pray in God's name: Your Kingdom come, Your will be done. See also Jn. 17:17; 2 Thess. 2:13b; 1 Pet. 1:22.

[41] Of course, I realize this is very much a simplified version of our internal function. For instance, I realize we are body and soul united, psychosomatic unities. We have emotions. We live in a socioeconomic context. I realize that we live in a spiritual realm.

BE MINDFUL OF YOUR MIND

We are primarily worshiping beings yet what, or who, we worship is informed by knowledge.[42] So, witness Paul on Mars Hill, "What you worship as unknown, this I proclaim to you" (Acts. 17:23). The problem is not that we are worshipers, but that we worship the *wrong* things. Thus, knowledge is essential, and I mean essential, nothing else will do. Knowledge, by the power of the Holy Spirit, brings new life through new, and true, worship. People will not be saved and transformed unless they hear and understand God's truth (cf. Rom. 10:9-18).[43]

Jonathan Edwards helps us here:

---

[42] Are former manner of life was corrupt through deceitful desires, misplaced and misinformed worship, yet we now put off that way of life (mortification) and put on the new way (vivification) through the renewal of our minds through the spirit of our minds (see Eph. 4:20-24 cf. Col. 3:1-17). We use to be confirmed to the passions of our former ignorance but we are told to be transformed through our minds. We are told to prepare our minds and set our hope on the one true God and His truth and not all the deceitful things that vie for our worship (see 1 Pet. 1:13-14 cf. 2 Pet. 1:5; Rom. 6:17). Thus, we purify our souls through obedience to the truth (1 Pet. 1:22).

[43] "No speech can be any means of grace, but by conveying knowledge... Therefore hearing is absolutely necessary to faith; because hearing is necessary to understanding" (Jonathan Edwards, "Christian Knowledge: or, The Importance and Advantage of a Thorough Knowledge of Divine Truth," 158 in the *The Works of Jonathan Edwards* vol. 2 [Carlisle, PA: The Banner of Truth Trust, 2009]). Jesus Himself tells us that hearing is not enough in itself. One must understand what is heard. When anyone *hears* the word of the kingdom but *does not understand it* then the evil one comes and snatches away what has been sown in his heart. (cf. Matt. 13:19).

BE MINDFUL OF YOUR MIND

There can be no love without knowledge. It is not according to the nature of the human soul, to love an object which is entirely unknown. The heart cannot be set upon an object of which there is no idea in the understanding. The reasons which induce the soul to love, must first be understood, before they can have a reasonable influence on the heart...

Such is the nature of man, that nothing can come at the heart but through the door of the understanding: and there can be no spiritual knowledge of that of which there is not first a rational knowledge.[44]

Thus, although we are primarily worshipers, our worship can be fundamentally (re)shaped at its core by the purposeful and intense implantation of knowledge. We, as Christians, seek for this knowledge to be thoroughly biblical and obtained by hard work and ultimately implanted by the Spirit for God's glory.

Because of the interconnectedness of knowledge, worship, and practice/habits we are told to think on, meditate on, percolate in, get God's truth deep into the core of our

---

[44] Edwards, "Christian Knowledge," 158.

being. This is so fundamental because where our treasure is our heart will be also (Matt. 6;21; Lk. 12:34) and out of our heart comes our life (Ecc. 10:2; Matt. 12:34-35; 15:18-19; Lk. 6:45). So, we must treasure the right thing.[45] We must purposely set our affections on Christ and His truth (cf. Rom. 8:5-6; Phil. 4:8-9; Col. 1:-2) and thus be habitually changed to reflect His image. This is how we use our minds to fight against enslaving sin.

In short, the mind is important because worship shapes our actions and our mind, through the Spirit's empowerment, can (re)shape our worship. So use your mind to stir up holy affections for the Lord and fight against deathly temptations.

THE CHRISTIAN MIND AND CHRISTIAN LIVING

The Christian mind is important because it leads to walking in freedom from sin. This is for various reasons. As we have seen, our mind—what we think on, know, understand —changes us by changing what or who we worship and to the degree that we worship. Knowledge, when seen in this light, is truly life-changing. Paul, previously Saul, is just

---

[45] "Being a disciple of Jesus is not primarily a matter of getting the right ideas and doctrines and beliefs into your head in order to guarantee proper behavior; rather, it's a matter of being the kind of person who *loves* rightly—who loves God and neighbor and is oriented to the world by the primacy of that love" (Smith, *Desiring the Kingdom,* 32-33).

BE MINDFUL OF YOUR MIND

one example of this. Paul's eyes were opened when he was blinded by the Messiah Jesus' glory. Paul thus worshiped Jesus. Then, he died for Jesus. Paul saw things anew (knowledge) and worshiped Jesus (worship) and thus was radically changed; changed in practice, habits, and in every way (Christian living).

It is when we abide in Christ, in part, through knowledge of Him, that we bear much fruit (Jn. 15:4 cf. 8:41; 15:10; Col. 3:16). Our cognition deeply affects Christian living. So, is your self-control slipping? Are you tempted to go back to the bottle or website? Maybe you ought to check your mind control? What are you thinking on? What are you teaching yourself? What are you loving?

What we sow in our minds we reap in our actions.[46] Or to say it another way, if we only eat ice cream and cotton candy we can't expect to be healthy. What we put in our bodies affects our bodies, and what we put in our minds affects our minds. Don't put junk in your mind.

As I have said, thinking for the Christian is not just theoretical, it is eminently practical. The Christian knows the truth and it sets them free (Jn. 8:32). Yet, the Christian doesn't just *know* truth, but reaches out with hands

---

[46] John R. W. Stott, *Your Mind Matters: The Place of the Mind in the Christian Life* (Downers Grove: InterVarsity Press, 2006), 58.

BE MINDFUL OF YOUR MIND

and a heart of love (cf. 1 Cor. 13:1-3; James 2:14-26). We are blessed not just by knowing the truth but by doing it (Jn. 13:17). Our minds inform our singing. We worship with our spirit and our mind (1 Cor. 14:15 cf. Eph. 5:15-20; Col. 3:16). Christian, your mind molds you—your worship, the way you live, and the way you die. It is important.

We are told at church, in books, and by all sorts of Christian leaders to read the Bible. But why? Because when the word of Christ dwells in us, makes its home in us, we are (trans)formed by it. It becomes our guide, our lamp to light the path (Ps. 119:105; Prov. 6:23), more than beer commercials, sitcoms, and the mall. Scripture, when we get it deep down into ourselves, will train us in righteousness and make us competent, equipped for every good work. The knowledge of God's truth leads to paths of righteousness, life, and truth; instead of foolishness, wickedness, and death.

Christian thinking is not to be cold. It is not to stay in the ivory tower. It is to come down with hands of love. Christian thinking must be the furnace driving the engine of love.[47] Thinking is very practical for the Christian, it is integrated into all of life. It is important at the inception and through to the conclusion. *Christian* thinking is vital because

---

[47] John Piper, *Think: The Life of the Mind and the Love of God* (Wheaton: Crossway, 2010), 54.

thinking is inevitable. The question is not will we think, it's will we think *Christianly*. Will we think in the right way and to the right end?

We must remember, knowledge is not the end in itself. If we have all knowledge and understand the inexplicable yet have not love we gain nothing (1 Cor. 13:2-3). We must remember that now we see in a mirror dimly, but we shall see face to face. Now we know in part; but we shall know fully, even as we have been fully known (1 Cor. 13:12).

Thus, briefly, we have seen that Christian thinking has a very practical impact on our fight against sin.

CONCLUSION

The Christian mind is important because (1) there is a huge precedence in Scripture for it, (2) it shapes and informs our worship, and thus (3) transforms and helps us fight against enslaving sin.

TAKE AWAY

- How can you use your mind in the fight against sin?
- Read an apologetic book.
- Resolve and make a game plan to think over a portion of Scripture.

8
THE FIGHT OF FAITH

INTRODUCTION
The fight of faith. The battle of belief. This is the war we wage. We overcome temptations and trials through faith (Heb. 11).

Our sanctification, our survival, is tethered to the anchor of our hope. If we are not anchored deep, we will be tossed to and fro. We will make shipwreck of our faith.

How do we cast anchor? How do we preserve in life's storms? How do we wage our warfare?

We do it, the Bible continually shows us, through faith, through biblical convictions. Yet, how do we have faith? Or how do we increase our faith? We will get to that most practical question. But, first, let's see (1) where it is that the Bible teaches this and (2) seek to understand how faith does this.

THE FIGHT OF FAITH

FAITH HELPS US FIGHT

First, the Bible teaches that faith not only saves, but also sanctifies. Our belief that brings us into the fold also keeps us there. This is seen in various places in Scripture, both Old Testament and New Testament. We'll take our example from 1 Peter.

God has caused us to be born again through faith (1 Pet. 1:3 cf. Jn. 1:13; 3:3-8; Eph. 2:4-5; Col. 2:13; Titus 3:5; James 1:18; 1 Pet. 1:23; 1 Jn. 2:29; 3:9; 4:7; 5:1, 4, 18); that is, salvation. Yet, faith also continues to work; it sanctifies us and makes us holy in practice. By God's power we are guarded *through faith* for salvation (1 Pet. 1:5 cf. Rom. 11:20). We see this worked out in 1 Peter 1. Peter says, "Having purified your souls by your obedience to the truth." We purify our souls because we believe the truth, because we have faith. Faith acts! It did for Peter; it did for Paul (cf. e.g. "the obedience of faith" Rom. 1:5; 16:26); it did for James (James 2:14-26), and it *should* for us.

Second, the Bible shows how it is that faith sanctifies and preserves us. Again, we will take our example from 1 Peter.

When we believe that we have a reason for hope (1 Pet. 3:15), we know that we are not following cleverly devised myths (2 Pet. 1: 15, 16), then we live accordingly. We, for example, "put away all malice and all deceit

THE FIGHT OF FAITH

and hypocrisy" (1 Pet. 2:1). It's simply the natural outcome of belief, or, that is, it should be.

So, for example, suppose I am exhausted from a long day's work. I come home, see the chair in the corner of the kitchen that's always beckoning me. It's made from solid hardwood. I got it when I worked at furniture store. I know it's solid. So, I sit down on it. I rest. I take my boots off.

However, suppose that chair was not made of hardwood. Suppose I did not get it from the furniture store at which I worked. Suppose I got it from a trash heap. I would then have much to question about its sturdiness. If I conjecture that it won't hold my weight, then I will not sit in it.

Why? Why do I sit in one chair and not the other? Because I have faith in the one and not the other. Faith, quite literally, moves us. That is why Peter talks about the "tested genuineness of your faith" (1 Pet. 1:7). Faith is testable. Is action wedded with our faith? Do we, so to speak, sit in the chair?

Active faith is seen in various places in Scripture. Thus, it says, *"when mindful of God,"* i.e. when one has faith, one is willing to endure sorrows (1 Pet. 2:19). We are even told to rejoice when we share in Christ's sufferings because then we will be blessed (1 Pet. 4:13-14; 5:4, 10). We can only rejoice at such things if we truly have faith. Paul also talks about the "obedience of faith" (Rom. 1:5; 16:26 cf. Acts 6:7) and Hebrews shows us that we endure all sorts of suffering and fight temptation "by faith" (Heb. 11: 4, 7, 8, 17, 24-26).

Faith radically changes us. Yet how can we have *more* faith?

HOW DO WE HAVE FAITH TO FIGHT?

How, practically, can we be firm in the faith? How can we persevere? How can we increase in faith? This is very important because as Isaiah says, "If you are not firm in the faith, you will not be firm at all" (Is. 1:6 cf. 1 Cor. 16:13).

As we fight to be firm in the faith, it's imperative that we have a holistic approach. The process of change, that is sanctification, is not a simplistic process. Here is one way of looking at the process: stimuli → thinking → emotions → actions = character (see Figure 3 below). I think we see this same type of schema in 2 Peter 1:5-11.

Actually, we see this all over Scripture. Jesus for instance said, "Love the LORD your God with all your heart, soul, mind, and strength" (cf. Mk. 12:30). Paul says, "Be transformed by the renewal of your mind" (Rom. 12:2) (cognitive), the Psalms say worship (e.g. Ps. 29:2) (emotive), other places say do righteousness (Jer. 22:3) (volitional).

THE FIGHT OF FAITH

We see that this is the very process that leads to revival in the book of Nehemiah. Cognitive understanding (see esp. Neh. 8:7-8) led to emotional experience (Neh. 8:9-12), which in turn led to action (confession, 9:1-37; and covenantal resolve, 9:38).

Ephesians tells us that instead of being tossed around by all sorts of things that make big promises but don't deliver, we must have convictions (Eph. 4:14-15). We must speak the truth, confess the truth, and hold close to the truth. Notice this is something we do together! We speak the truth to each other. We remind each other of the gospel so that when temptation comes we won't be like a child in the ocean with big waves crashing in (cf. Eph. 4:14-15; Heb. 3:12-13; 10:24-25; Eph. 5:19; Col. 3:16).

We persevere in the faith as we think on God's truth (1 Cor. 15:1; 2 Thess. 2:15). God's truth is one of the positive forms of stimuli. It transforms (cf. Jn. 17:17). We have faith not through some nebulous and opaque placement of faith. God uses means. He uses knowledge of various things. He uses experiences. He uses conversations with friends. He uses Scripture. He uses the gathered worship of the church. Thus, faith is a fight. And continuing in the faith is a fight. This is because there are things we must do. God uses means to accomplish His ends.

THE FIGHT OF FAITH

What are some of the means that God uses to accomplish the end of preserving us in the faith? How can we be firm in the faith?

First, God uses our mind (cognition) (cf. Prov. 4:23; 23:7; 2 Cor. 10:5; Rom. 12:2; Eph. 4:22-24; Phil. 4:8). We prepare our *minds* for action (1 Pet. 1:13) and set our hope fully on the grace that was brought to us at the revelation of the Messiah. We are supposed to be able to give a defense for the reason we have hope (1 Pet. 3:15). We must use our minds and remind ourselves of truth so we will be firmly established (2 Pet. 1:12). We must recall that we do not follow "cleverly devised myths" (2 Pet. 1: 15, 16).

We must use our minds! In fact, God "has granted to us all things that pertain to life and godliness, through the *knowledge* of Him" (2 Pet. 1:3). In this category, God often uses the means of apologetics, contemplation on Scripture, study of devotional texts, and so forth to transform. Our cognitive belief has practical impact (when it is true belief). According to 1 Peter 1:13, "you believe in Him and [thus] rejoice with joy that is inexpressible" (In this case, we see an emotional impact).

Second, God uses our emotions (emotive). For example, when we have prepared minds, minds set on hope (1 Pet. 1:13), we are soberminded. We have emotions but they are grounded in truth. So, we have due fear of the

THE FIGHT OF FAITH

LORD because we believe, with our *mind*, that He is our Father and will judge us according to our deeds (1 Pet. 1:17 cf. Rom. 11:20). Thus, we, because of cognitive and emotive reasons, reform our actions. In this category, God often uses community, worship, meditation, etc. to transform.

Third, God uses our actions (volition). Once we have right thinking and thus right emotions, we have, or should have, right actions. We should no longer be "conformed to the passions of [our] former ignorance" (1 Pet. 1:14). We should no longer practice our "futile ways" (1 Pet. 1:18). Notice, "ignorance" and "futile" are both cognitive-type terms which are worked out in the volitional realm. So, Peter says, "As He who called you is holy (both cognitive and emotive), be holy in all your conduct (volitional)" (1 Pet. 1:15). God uses worship, community, refraining from certain unholy practices, acts of charity, and so forth to transform us.

In this whole schema that I have sought to lay out, there is a back and forth. We should not fix lines where none is fixed. They intersect at many points and continue, like wires, woven together. Knowledge presses emotion and action forward and builds character. Yet, action (e.g. forcing one's self out of bed early to read Scripture) affects our cognitive and emotive side.

THE FIGHT OF FAITH

As I have said, there is a reciprocal connection between what we think, feel, and consciously do. What we think on and how we think, what we feel and how we interact with what we feel, and what we do and how we do it shapes us into who we are. Thus, we must seek to evaluate how we think, feel, and do in light of God's truth.

So, saving faith is a continuing faith and an active faith. It makes use of means. That's why we resist the devil by being "firm in the faith" (1 Pet. 5:9). Of course, we must remember, faith is not static. Neither does it stagnate. For God uses means.

> *"Therefore, brothers, be all the more diligent to confirm your calling and election, for if you practice these qualities you will never fall. For in this way there will be richly provided for you an entrance into the eternal kingdom of our Lord and Savior Jesus Christ" (2 Pet. 1:10-11).*

TAKE AWAY

- We must fight with faith. We must not give in to the lies of temptation because we believe the Lord's promises and truth.

THE FIGHT OF FAITH

- How can you "beef up" your fight of faith?
- In the Bible we see different times when a large stone or pile of rocks were used as reminders of the way God delivered His people. Samuel, for example, took a big stone, named it, and said, "Till now the Lord has helped us" (1 Sam. 7:12). These monuments increased peoples faith by reminding them of what God did. You don't have to pile up rocks but what can serve as a monument for you? What can you purposely remember that will strengthen your faith when it's weak? Maybe a Bible verse in the dashboard of your car? Maybe you should write down how God saved you? I'm not sure. But do something. Erect a monument. Remember what the Lord has done. Strive to strengthen your faith.

PART THREE: THE TRANSFORMATION STEPS

"I therefore,... urge you to walk in a manner worthy of the calling to which you have been called."
– Ephesians 4:1

"Beloved, we are God's children now, and what we will be has not yet appeared; but we know that when He appears we shall be like Him, because we shall see Him as He is."
– 1 John 3:2

"Let us consider how to stir up one another to love and good works, not neglecting to meet together, as is the habit of some, but encouraging one another."
– Hebrews 10:24-25

9
DON'T LISTEN TO LIES

INTRODUCTION
Many in the early and exciting stage of addiction are naive and completely oblivious to the crushing evil that will soon engulf them. Now they feel. Feel like they have never felt. Alive. So alive. Yet, soon they will be numb. Walking, but dead. As C.S. Lewis says, the safest road to hell is the one that doesn't have road signs telling of the destination.48 The one that seems safe enough. The one that softly descends until it's barely noticed that the road descended into the depths of hell.

In the vicious cycle of addiction, guilt often drags the tortured soul deeper and

---

[48] See C. S. Lewis, *The Screwtape Letters* (New York: Macmillan, 1980), 56.

deeper down into despair and slavery. In this state it can be hard to hear God's voice. Sometimes He has to shake you to wake you.

One friend wrote this to me from prison: "Know this Paul, I'm right where I need to be so don't think I'm sad at all! Shoot! I'm truly thankful & blessed to know he (God) loves me enough to sit me down and be still." Later he said, "With Jesus I can be forgiven! From East to West! ...I'm clean (no drugs) getting my health back, thinking clearly & most of all I'm right with God!!"

Sometimes God has to do sit us down, even put us in prison, so we will wake up from our stupor and listen. Will we listen and deal with the real problem? Or will we say there's not a problem. Or will we blame our addiction on something else? I hope we will wake up and stop listening to lies!

A LOOK AT PROVERBS 7

Your lust, your addiction, your lying, your sin *will* kill you. Yet, it's easy to forget that truth when we're entangled in a web of temptations lies.

Proverbs 7 has done a good job reminding me of the lies of sin. I am looking at that page in my Bible right now and it looks tired and tatted from all the work that it's done on my heart. I encourage you to put this book down and read Proverbs 7 (I mean really how often

DON'T LISTEN TO LIES

does an author ask you to put his book down?! So I would suggest you do it).

Proverbs 7 is old, around 3,000 years old. So how does it apply? First, what is the text addressing? Look at Proverbs 7:10-12. Who is the woman in this passage? She is a seductress, a temptress.

So why should you care? Because this passage is talking about *your* sin. No, you may not be running after a seductress but you crave something. Proverbs here is not merely addressing the temptation of adultery but temptation in general. Proverbs uses adultery as a case study. We will just have to plug in our own situation. This passage applies to us all. Listen. Because this, as we will see, is a matter of life and death.

We must keep God's Word and keep away from sin. We must tattoo God's Word on our heart (Prov. 7:1-5). Verse 2a says "keep my commandments and live" but in order to keep them we must know them. That is why we must treasure up God's Word and keep it as the apple of our eye.

We must keep God's word always before us. We must even etch it onto our heart. It is one thing to write something down, another to use a *Sharpie*, but another thing altogether to engrave something. We must hide God's Word so thoroughly in our hearts that it will be permanently upon us, like a tattoo. When God's word is bond on our hearts and wisdom

DON'T LISTEN TO LIES

is our close friend *then* it will keep us from the forbidden woman. When we know God's Word we will see the lies of lust and the lies of addictive substances (cf. Ps. 119:11; Jn. 17:17). We need the sword of God's Word to fight against temptation.

Proverbs 7 teaches us that we must run and hide from sin (Prov. 7:6-12). It tells us that the young man in chapter 7 is lacking sense, is stupid, and unwise. But why? Because he is passing "near her corner" (v. 8). Ok? What's the big deal with that?

I am in the army and I have gone through tons of training on how to cross a road, go under bridges, and around corners when driving a Humvee. Why? Because they are danger spots. In fact, if these spots can be avoided we are to avoid them. It is not wise to go into these situations if you can avoid them because it is in these situations that the enemy is near and waiting to ambush. If mounted Humvees seek to avoid the "danger spots" we must avoid them all together.

We must not go "near her corner." Whatever "near the corner" means for us. For some it means no smartphone, for others it means no cash on hand, and avoiding certain parts of town.

We must flee from sin (1 Cor. 6:18; 2 Tim. 2:22; Prov. 5:8; 6:27). Too often we try to reason ourselves out of this. We say, "If I don't hang out with my friend how will they

DON'T LISTEN TO LIES

get saved?" Yet the real question is, "If I keep falling into temptation in front of them, how will they get saved?" It us true that Jesus ministered to prostitutes but that ministry is not for everyone. It is true that drug dealers and drug users need Christ but if you're tempted to sell or do drugs that is probably not the ministry that God has for you, at least at this point in your life.

Imagine you're on a diet; you're trying not to eat sweets to lose a few pounds. Let me ask you though, before you go on this diet, do you fill your freezer with ice cream and your cupboards with chocolate? If you do, you are foolish. Or you're just not serious about your diet. Yet how often do we do this very thing with our addiction? With pornography? With drugs? You might say to yourself, "I don't want to use tonight. I'm just going to hangout for a little bit..." But your actions say something completely different.

We may *say* we don't want to keep taking pills, smoking joints, but is that true if we keep going to that person's house? We don't want to do so many things, *supposedly*. If solders had mindset in wartime today, they would be dead; the enemy would kill them. They take extreme precautions to avoid enemy ambush and so must we.

We must not walk near her corner. We must be on guard and avoid "the corner." You know your corner. You know where

DON'T LISTEN TO LIES

temptation gets you. If you can avoid that corner, you'll be on the way to win the battle.

I, basically, never watch movies or TV. This is *my* personal conviction for *me*. This is one way I seek to avoid the corner (see Prov. 7:7-8 cf. 5:8). This may not be your "corner" or "danger spot," that's fine. I understand. I only give this for an example.

When I was in college I worked as a security officer. When I got to the guard shack, I was

very intentional about turning off the TV right away. I didn't want to *react* but *pre-act*.

If we are near the corner, we are foolish (Prov. 6:27). We must be proactive and avoid the corner. We must practice radical amputation. We must be willing to not drive on certain roads, look the other way when passing Hooters (I do this!), take a baseball bat to the laptop. We must do what it takes.

We must not listen to the lies (7:13-27) "She seizes him and kisses him" and promises him sexual delight. She says "Come, let us take our fill of love till morning; let us delight ourselves with love." She says there won't be consequences, no one will find out, my husband is not home. She says, "Come with me we'll have fun and no one will know.

Is this not the lie of lust? The lie that we can drink in lust and it doesn't matter; there are no consequences and it hurts no one and is in fact normal. Temptation always make

DON'T LISTEN TO LIES

big promises, whether it's a substance or pornography.

At first, she, the temptation, may look good. She may drip honey, but in the end, she is bitter as wormwood, sharp as a two-edged sword. Her feet go down to death; her steps follow the path to hell (Prov. 5:3-5). The river of temptation has a strong current and it will carry you along until your terrible fall unless you fight it and escape its grasp.

Temptation says, "Come, let us take our fill of love till morning; let us delight ourselves with love" (v. 18). Is this not what our temptation sounds like? And notice, it promises no consciences, "My husband is not at home" (v. 19); no one will ever know, so it doesn't matter. Let's apply this concept to dieting. No one may ever know that you ate that ice cream that night when you were all alone but your life will show it or at least your waistline will. Plus, once you have that one bit of ice cream the next one doesn't seem so bad, in fact, it seems really good. Temptation promises pleasure and delivers it, for a time. Yet it is only for a time (see v. 21-23).

Someone I knew is a prime example of this. I had no idea my friend was addicted to pornography until after his death. I went to his house to help clean up some of his stuff. It was a mess. We carried out and burned load after load of pornographic magazine. It was sickening. It literally made me sick to my stomach. The event actually helped me see the sick and distorted thing that pornography and lust truly are. It turns people into monsters. In the end lust will kill. Yes there are consequences. I didn't know it until not very long ago but that same "friend" molested a close friend of mine. Lust is the way of death even if she promises delight.

However, it is not just lust that brings death and depravity, it is sin. All sin. Your sin. Don't let yourself off the hook here. You may not feel tempted to molest a young girl but what about that lie you told yesterday? What about those bottles you're going to drink tonight? We all have lies we hear. We must answer them with God's truth.

We must remember that if we follow her (our temptress) it will be as an ox to the slaughter (Prov. 7:22). As surely as the ox going to the slaughter brings death so will our sin bring death. If we follow our temptation, we will be like a mouse going to the cheese in the mousetrap. We may get the cheese but it will kill us. If the mouse knew that the mousetrap would kill it surely it would stay clear. Brothers and sisters, we know sin *will kill us* and yet so often we fail to stay clear. Let's be wiser then mice! Let's avoid the deadly trap.

We have seen through God's Word that sin is a trap that brings death. So let's avoid it.

DON'T LISTEN TO LIES

If we don't it will cost us our family, our ministry, and our life.

Listen to wisdom, obey God's Word because "many victims she has laid low." Lust is pictured here as a dreadful mighty warrior and we are told not to fight with her but to avoid her because she has destroyed many. Bible students, pastors, and professors are included in this "many." In fact, she can, and will take us all down if we don't avoid her. Brothers and sisters, sin, grave sin, is not beyond me and is not beyond you. Alcoholism, drug addiction, or whatever it may be is not beyond you.

> *"And now, O sons, listen to me,*
> *and be attentive to the words of my mouth.*
> *Let not your heart turn aside to her ways;*
> *do not stray into her paths,*
> *for many a victim has she laid low,*
> *and all her slain are a mighty throng.*
> *Her house is the way to Sheol,*
> *going down to the chambers of death"* (Prov. 7:24-27).

Don't listen to sins' lies! Hide God's Word in your heart and run from temptation!

Will this woman, will this sin, be the death of you? Or will you do everything in your power to flee from her?

DON'T LISTEN TO LIES

All have sinned, *everyone*, and fallen short of the glory of God. None is righteous, not even you. We have all followed our temptation, whatever it may be. We are all like the ox going to the slaughter. We are all on the path to Sheol. Is not this true? Is not the wages of sin death?

Yes it is, but praise God, Jesus has died in our place! The wages of sin is death. But! But the *gift* of God is eternal life! Brother and sisters you and *me* deserve death, slaughter. But, in while we were yet sinners, Christ died for us! For *us*! God promises those who have faith in Him eternal life instead of the death we deserve. He not only gives eternal life but also an abundant and free life here.

Many of you are already in the shackles of sin. You've been entangled in the seductress' lies, whatever those lies may be; you're like a mouse in a trap. You may have the cheese but your caught, going nowhere, and dying. Can you be free? Free from the shackles of your addictive sin? God says you can! He is able to help those who are tempted. Trust in Jesus for salvation and look to Jesus in your sanctification.

We are free—no longer slaves of sin!—through Christ! We no longer inherit death but eternal life. Yet, now, we serve as slaves to our *good* Master, God Himself. We now serve a good Master, with good rewards, but we *must* serve Him (See Rom. 6:20-23).

TAKE AWAY

- Do you realize that your sin, if not avoided, will lead to death? As John Owen has famously said, Kill sin or it will kill you!
- God's Word has an important function in keeping us from seductress temptations (cf. Prov. 7:1-5). Read Proverbs 7.

10
REMEMBER, SIN IS *NOT* GOOD

INTRODUCTION

In our fight against our enslaving sin, it is imperative that we remember that "sin is not good." I hope that phrase is not news to you. I hope it's not some big revelation. However, in another sense, I hope it is a big revelation. I hope you will see the profound nastiness of sin (cf. Ps. 97:10; 101:3; Rom. 12:9).

The whole point of this chapter is for us to look at how bad sin is and remember that Satan is the great deceiver and father of lies (Rev. 12:9; Jn. 8:44). Our temptations make big promises but as we saw in the previous chapter they fall short and lead to death.

REMEMBER, SIN IS *NOT* GOOD

Satan's desire is to destroy. Jesus longs to give abundant life (cf. Matt. 23:37; Jn. 3:16; 10:10). However, we often get those two truths backwards. We think our temptation offers abundant life and Jesus offers restrictions. This chapter is written to combat that false thinking.

SIN *LOOKS* REALLY GOOD

Sin is ingenuine. It makes big promises but never delivers. Truly the world and sin promise happiness and fulfillment. They promise to give us meaning and comfort. But they only take them away. The world and sin give us poisoned pills wrapped in sugar.[49]

Satan sells us lies and blinds our eyes. He would have us contended with filth and miss the glorious Lord who is worthy of all praise and can satisfy our longing soul. Truly Satan is crafty and subtle in his lies (recall the way he talked to Eve; Gen. 3:1ff cf. Lk. 4:1). He is a lion that is crouched low (1 Pet. 5:8). We don't always see him but his desire is to destroy.

Satan is the god of this world (2 Cor. 4:4; Rev. 2:13) and his worship leads to curses and hatred of neighbor. In him is death and he is the futility of man; whoever lives in his influence shall perish and not have life

---

[49] See Thomas Watson, *Heaven Taken by Storm* (Morgan, PA: Soli Deo Gloria Publications, 1997), 44.

REMEMBER, SIN IS *NOT* GOOD

(reverse of Jn. 1:4; 3:16). The world sits on the back of this evil beast of death (cf. Rev. 17:3). The world doesn't know it but all people follow the course the beast has set, and it's a funeral procession, that leads to the grave (cf. Eph. 2:1-3).

So Satan, the lord of this age, is rightly called the "deceiver of the whole world," the "father of lies" (Rev. 12:9; Jn. 8:44 cf. Rev. 13:14; 18:23; 19:20; 20:3; 2 Cor. 11:3; 2 Thess. 2:9-11; 1 Tim. 2:14). He is a dragon that smites many hosts yet not by the fire of his mouth but by the damning effects of his lies. And what do you expect his children to say? "They promise freedom, but they themselves are slaves" (2 Pet. 2:19 cf. Jer. 6:14; 8:11; Matt. 24:24; Jn. 8:44; Rom. 16:18; Eph. 4:14; 2 Pet. 2). Those that know not Christ are blind and would have us wander around in darkness too (cf. 2 Cor. 4:4-6). Satan and his children boast of good, but it's all tainted, and leads to death (cf. Prov. 5:1-6; 7).

Thus, sin is not good because although it can *look* good, it's not. It damns and destroys the good world God made. The de-creation voice of Satan pulls us toward death and non-being (cf. Jer. 4:23-27). It may *sound* good, as it did to Eve, but it is anything but good. It destroys. It curses and creates confusion. It sends us, guilty, out of Eden, where our good remains, and into Gehenna.

REMEMBER, SIN IS *NOT* GOOD

SIN IS THE UNMAKING OF MAN AND A MANIFOLD OF BEAUTIES

This world cries out like ripe fruit, "I'm good! Eat me! Indulge yourself..." However, much of the fruit here, as in the Garden, leads to cataclysmic clashes, with God, yourself, and humanity. It looks good and some of it is. But much of it has an infectious parasite on it. It's hard, but not impossible, to consume it without getting "sick."

In Genesis 3:1-24 we see the Fall of humanity. We see various forms of death given birth to. We see "'an ever-growing avalanche of sin, a continually widening chasm between man and God'. It progresses from disobedience, to murder, to indiscriminate killing, to titanic lust, to total corruption, and uncontrolled violence."[50] Sin truly brings a litany of death. "Disease, genetic disorders, famine, natural disasters, aging, and death itself are as much the result of sin as are oppression, war, crime, and violence. We have lost God's *shalom*—physically, spiritually, socially, psychologically, culturally. Things now fall

---

[50] Revd Victor James Johnson, "Illustrating Evil – The Effect of the Fall as seen in Genesis 4-11," 57 in *Melanesian Journal of Theology* 11-1&2 (1995).

REMEMBER, SIN IS *NOT* GOOD

apart."[51] Sin opens Pandora's box and unleashes a horde of evil.

We have marred more than the mediocre; we have marred the Michelangelos of the world. We have marred superb beauty and made it unbelievably hideous. Yet, if we see something that is less hideous we look at it as a wonder. Why? Because this world is so tainted and steeped in sin and the effects of sin.

To illustrate, if I ruin a "masterpiece" that my son made with paper, glue, and crayons, the ramifications will be far less than if I destroy the Mona Lisa. Well, creation was intended to be a Mona Lisa; that is, it was intended to be supremely glorious. God's creation was intended to be good, beautiful, and aesthetically pleasing to our senses, emotions, and intellect beyond what we can imagine. And so the ramifications of the destruction of such beauty are greater. We often think of this world as the way *it is* not as the way it was *intended to be*. If we could see a glimpse of what the Great Creator had in mind for His masterpiece, then we'd see that we "paved paradise and put up a parking lot." We essentially killed a thousand Beethovens and blared white noise. We backfilled the

---

[51] Timothy Keller, *The Reason for God: Belief in an Age of Skepticism* (New York: Penguin Group, 2008), 177. "Disunion with God is reflected in disunion with others and with oneself" (Johnson, *Foundations of Soul Care*, 466).

REMEMBER, SIN IS *NOT* GOOD

Grand Canyon with gravel. We burned a hundred museums of art. We scorched our taste buds off our tongue. We took a wrecking ball to all the wonders of the world and razed a thousand gorgeous cities. In short, through our "war crimes," we, as humanity, deserve death. We have brought cataclysmic chaos to the world.

Sin is not a light thing. We, as humans, were created in the image of God. We were to be *like* Christ, God in flesh (cf. Gen. 1:26-27). The world was meant to be supremely glorious, peaceful, and loving but instead it is disgusting and understandably repugnant to God. So, as we try to grasp the wonder of what has been marred we can begin to understand how serious the situation is and how terrible sin is.

Thus, sin is not good because it is the unmaking of man and a manifold of beauties.

SIN IS A REBELLION *AND* A RAMPAGE

Sin is immoral. It is an act against God. It is a transgression against God's law. But not only His law but also His *good* plan. Sin is not merely immoral or highhanded treason it is also a rampage because it is mad, meaning foolish, a form of insanity. It goes against good sense. It is a rampage because sin destroys the good.

REMEMBER, SIN IS *NOT* GOOD

We have all seen the pain and sorrow that moral degradation has wrought in our lives. We see it, for instance, in sins of others against us and those close to us. We see it in sins which we have sinned against others. We see it in the world at large (e.g. my parents were divorced, a very close friend of mine was molested as a child, and a friend of mine that struggled with drug-addiction committed suicide). There is, for sure, a law written on all our hearts, we go against it to the shame and suffering of humanity; and yet, we all do indeed go against it.

Humanity has and needs a moral standard. This points us to the Creator who gave it to us when He created us in His image. However, it also points us to the Fall. We all fail to measure up to the standard. We can all think of a hypothetical world where everyone followed these standards and where the result was great happiness. Yet, this is not the case. We do not follow these good (innate) standards. How odd. We know the good we ought to do, or at least that there is "a good," and yet we fail to do it.

Sin leads to terrible depravity, hopelessness, and disregard for humanity or anything good. This is vividly portrayed, for example, in Cormac McCarthy's post-apocalyptic book *The Road*. We don't want to suffer what is portrayed there. We don't even want to think of the horrors of Dachau and

REMEMBER, SIN IS *NOT* GOOD

Auschwitz. We all know the wickedness of Adolf Hitler, Pol Pot, and Joseph Kony. Yet perhaps their nearly unbelievable atrocities allow us to belittle (in our conscience) our own wickedness. However, even if our sin is so-called "low-grade wickedness" it is the equivalent of their sin, just on a micro level. It has the same seed, though perhaps it hasn't come to full bloom yet.

What must be realized is that *all* sin is a movement towards un-creation. In C.S. Lewis' words, through sin man becomes the "unman." Through sin everything that was very good (see Gen. 1:3, 10, 12, 18, 21, 25, 31) becomes cursed instead. Sin covers beauty, boasts in badness, and hides from the supreme joy we all seek. Sin is a rampage.

Sin is a leech and parasite. It lives off of and feeds on life and vitality. And it kills it. Bleeding it away little by little until the carrier is completely eaten away and destroyed. Note that this death, though complete, can be imperceptible.

Sin leads to de-creation as well as desecration. Humans were made in God's own image yet through sin that image has literally been put into dirt; man becomes dirt and ashes from whence he came (hence de-creation) (cf. Jer. 17:13). From perfection to

REMEMBER, SIN IS *NOT* GOOD

misdirection, from *shalom*[52] to shattering. Everything has come undone. The creation groans with longing. Sin is not merely moral. It is the decay of all things. Sin wrought a wreck and we are still wheeling and writhing in pain.

Thus, sin is not good not only because it is moral rebellion against a good and all-powerful God but also because it is a rampage against His good creation.

SIN IS HUMANITIES DEATH WISH

I was always told growing up that it's not good to do bad things. And for a time I was content with that. It didn't need to be explained to me. However, as time has gone on and temptations have increased, or at least my perception of them, I find it helpful to understand and remind myself of why "it's not good to do bad things."

Obviously, "it's not good to do bad things" because it doesn't please God. But why doesn't it please God? Why are bad things bad? We see from reflection on Scripture that bad things are bad because they are not in

---

[52] "In the Bible, shalom means *universal flourishing, wholeness, and delight...* a state of affairs that inspires joyful wonder as its Creator and Savior opens doors and welcomes the creatures in whom he delights. Shalom, in other words, is the way things ought to be" (Cornelius Plantinga Jr., *Not the Way It's Supposed to Be: A Breviary of Sin* [Grand Rapids, MI: Eerdmans, 1995], 10; italics original).

accord with God's character and, thus, apart from being bad they do not finally work with the way things are. In short, they are against the universe. Against existence. Against the way things are. Against the way things work. This is because God is good, supremely good. And creation is meant to operate in a certain way. Sin, evil, and bad are not innate within God's good creation. They don't "work" and will one day soon be expelled from the whole system. Then, and only then, will all things be put right and made new.

The consequence of sin is not arbitrarily imposed; it is instead the inevitable outworking of the implications of sin.[53] Turning away from God is like a diver cutting off the air to his breathing tube, it's unplugging your own life support.[54] The consequence of turning from the Lord is built in. And it's been that way from the beginning. "On the day you eat of it, you will surely die." Adam and Eve died a thousand little deaths before they took their last breaths.

To turn from God, to sin, is not only wrong but also foolish. Why? Because "God is our final good, our maker and savior, the one in whom alone our restless hearts come to

---

[53] Anthony N. S. Lane, "Lust: the human person as affected by disordered desires" 35 in EQ 78.1 [2006], 21-35.

[54] N. T. Wright, *Evil and the Justice of God* (Downers Grove: InterVarsity Press, 2006), 109.

REMEMBER, SIN IS *NOT* GOOD

rest. To rebel against God is to saw of the branch that supports us."[55]

Sin is humanity's death wish in every way.[56] To be separated from God is to die, physically and spiritually. Human flourishing, true shalom, is bound up with God. Apart from union with God, we can seek but we won't find.

The world is a dichotomy. It is two paths. The wise and the foolish. New creation and de-creation. Damnation and liberation. Life and death. Hell and heaven. Where, in a very real sense, are you going?

Thus, sin is not good because it is innately against human flourishing.[57] Sin is not good because it is humanity's death wish in every sense.

---

[55] Plantinga, *Not the Way It's Supposed to Be*, 123. "Sin dissipates us in futile—and self-destructive—projects. Sin hurts other people and grieves God, but it also corrodes *us*. Sin is a form of self-abuse" (Ibid., 124). "Sin against God is therefore outrageous folly: it's like pulling the plug on your own resuscitator" (Ibid., 125-26). Thus "because it is futile, because it is vain, because it is unrealistic, because it spoils good things, sin is a prime form of folly" (Ibid., 126).

[56] "The association of sin with physical and spiritual death runs like a spine through Scripture and Christian tradition" (Plantinga, *Not the Way It's Supposed to Be*, 47).

[57] "Human flourishing" rather is "the same thing as glorifying God and enjoying him forever" (Ibid., 37-38).

SIN BRINGS A TYPE OF LIVING HELL

"A trail of mutilated frogs lay along the edge of the island." This is the sad result of sin. In C. S. Lewis' book *Perelandra*, Weston, now the "unman," leaves a trail of mutilated frogs. Weston is the epicenter of evil. He is wholehearted evil, a predecessor to the Miserific Vision.

Yet, Weston, the "unman," is just a concentrated picture of what we saw with Adolf Hitler and his regime. It is a picture from a different angle of the mutilation that lays in the wake of Planned Parenthood. When we anonymously try to create our own utopia we leave a trail of mutilation. Whether we listen to the Nazi idea or the Planned Parenthood idea that says, with our culture, "have it your way," "listen to your heart," "do what feels right." When we "have it our way," "listen to our heart," and "do what feels right," then "might will make right" because there will be no higher authority and we may just have a reincarnation of the atrocities of Dachau and Auschwitz. We might just have people "aborting" "clumps of cells" in their wombs because that is just what they want to do, it is what is convenient; we might just have "doctors" sell "clumps of cells" as *human* organs. We "might" just have 54,559,615 lives lost through gruesome child sacrifice (abortion) in the USA; a number that can

REMEMBER, SIN IS *NOT* GOOD

seem to make insignificant the 407,300 lives lost by Americans as a result of WWII.

Truly, as much as we think we can, we can't "have our cake and eat it too." We can't indulge in sin and also think it won't bring consequences. Sin, since the beginning, has been accompanied with consequences. We can't, for example, indulge in pornography as individuals or as a society and not have an avalanche of abominations overtake us. When we treat humans as sexual objects to be exploited that is sadly what they become, and so human sex trafficking and child abduction ensue.

To quote an unlikely source, Friedrich Nietzsche said in *Beyond Good and Evil* that philosophy always creates a world in its own image, it cannot do anything different. When we create a world where morality doesn't exist, then in a very real way morality doesn't exist, at least, that's how people live. In this world each will do what is right in his own eyes, might will make right, and atrocities will flourish. Various attempts at the "Final Solution"[58] will abound, and so will death and desolation.

---

[58] The "Final Solution" was the Nazi ploy to systematically exterminate the Jewish population through genocide. What I am saying here is that there will be various other hellish "solutions" that will be offered to humanity. Yet, they likewise will fall disastrously short and only unleash a torrent of pain and wickedness. Witness the deaths in the name of "utopian" communism.

REMEMBER, SIN IS *NOT* GOOD

We reap what we sow philosophically, so right now we're reaping a whole host of debauchery as a society. Could it be that teachings have been tainted and thus a litany of death ensues? Maybe it is time to re-explore worldviews and their corresponding idea of human flourishing and the ability that they have to match reality to their claims.

Human bodies ripped from the womb, mutilated, and sold, and the world doesn't bat an eye. Sad; yet not surprising in our naturalistic, hedonistic, secular day. Moral decay happens when something other than God is our ultimate good (cf. Rom. 1). Humanity spirals out of control and implodes in on itself whenever we make gods in our own image; whether infanticide in the Roman Empire, Auschwitz during the Nazi regime, or rampant abortion today. When we decipher and dictate anonymously and subjectively what is good and prosperous for ourselves and society, we damn ourselves and those around us. We, so to speak, eat again of the forbidden fruit and cast ourselves out of Eden. We fall into a pit we ourselves dug. We kill Abel, revel in Babel, and inculcate innumerable evils. We make life a sort of living hell; picture the living, walking, and tortured skeletons from the horrors of concentration camps engraved in our memories.

Sin creates a sort of living hell.

REMEMBER, SIN IS *NOT* GOOD

SIN, RESULTING IN THE FALL, EXPLAINS HUMANITIES WRETCHEDNESS AND YET GREATNESS

The philosopher Blaise Pascal lamented, "What sort of freak is man! How novel, how monstrous, how chaotic, how paradoxical, how prodigious! Judge of all things, feeble earthworm, repository of truth, sink of doubt and error, the glory and refuse of the universe!"[59]

> *The inexplicable phenomenon of mankind: unquestionably corrupt, subject to inconstancy, boredom, anxiety and selfishness, doing anything in the waking hours to divert the mind from human wretchedness, yet showing the vestiges of inherent greatness in the mind's realization of this condition. Mankind is also finite, suspended between twin infinities revealed by telescope and microscope, and aware of an inner emptiness which the finite world fails to satisfy. No philosophy makes sense of this. No moral system makes us better or happier. One*

---

[59] Pascal, *Pensees*, (131).

> *hypothesis alone, creation in the divine image followed by the fall, explains our predicament and, through a redeemer and mediator with God, offers to restore our rightful state.*[60]

Human greatness split the atom, human wretchedness uses the same to kill millions of people. A great, though wretched, leader, Adolf Hitler, will lead a nation to slaughter millions. A great leader, Winston Churchill, will lead a nation in their defense. As much as we are great, we bare God's image. As much as we are wretched, we bare Satan's. Ashok Gadgil,[61] with his intelligence, will fight for cures; others will inject poison. Humanity is simultaneously great and wretched. What explains this paradox? We all innately sense, it but why is it here?

Humanity is fallen. So we cannot neatly divide the line between good and evil. We cannot say all the bad people on the left and all the good people on the right. We are all mixed together.[62] We are made in God's image and thus can do fantastic things and fantastic good but we have been marred by

---

[60] D.G. Preston, "Pascal, Blaise," 492 in *New Dictionary of Theology,* ed. Sinclair B. Ferguson, David F. Wells, and J.I. Packer (Downers Grove, IL: InterVarsity Press, 1988).

[61] See e.g. https://youtu.be/6ccTlh7jaGw.

[62] Wright, *Evil and the Justice of God,* 38.

the Fall and often reflect Satan so we can also do acts of unbelievable wickedness.

Thus, sin is not good because it wreaks havoc on our greatness, on the fact that we were created in the image of God, and distorts it to evil ends. How sad that we who are capable of exploring the limitless expanse of the sea, the mind, space, and biology so often content ourselves with razing and rioting. How sad that though we as humanity are capable of such good, there is such grave injustice. I've read, for example, that a woman born in parts of South Africa is more likely to be raped then to learn to read.[63] This surely should not be!

SIN LEADS TO ENSLAVEMENT

Sin is like Gollum's ring. It enslaves and destroys. It looks so good but ends in lava.

Truly, what we worship will either ruin us or reunite us to the purpose of our existence.[64] And we *all* worship something. Worship is not merely something we *do*. It's who we *are*.[65] We are innately worshipers.

---

[63] How strange and how sad that we hate the thought of this and yet many still struggle with the wickedness of pornography. Most of humanity hates the thought of human trafficking but yet enjoys the very things that feed that market.

[64] Cf. G. K. Beale, *We Become what we Worship: A Biblical Theology of Idolatry* (Downers Grove: InterVarsity Press, 2008.).

[65] See Noel Doe, *Created for Worship: From Genesis to Revelation to You* (Ross-shire, Scotland: Mentor, 2009), 20.

REMEMBER, SIN IS *NOT* GOOD

Yet when we aim at the wrong thing, worship the wrong thing, and thus deprive God of His glory, He deprives us of ours[66] and we end up empty and doing all manner of wickedness. This is woven into the fabric of the universe, of our very existence.

We *will* worship. That's not the question. The question is who or what will we worship and to what end. What will be the result?

One catechism asks, "With what design did God create man?" The answer: that we should know God, love and glorify Him, and so be happy forever.[67] Truly we are to worship God not merely because He commands us to but because that is what we were created to do. Worship is inevitable.[68] It *will* and *is* happening. The question is not will you worship, but what? And what will it lead to?

Will it damn you and lead to enslavement? Or will it bring eternal shalom and human flourishing (i.e. true cross-cultural human flourishing not the mere individualistic perception of flourishing) (recall Rom. 1 and 6)? Is it true or is it false?

When we worship the LORD we are going with the grid that is innately ingrained within us since the beginning. This is innate within

---

[66] cf. Doe, *Created for Worship*, 29.

[67] Longer Catechism of the Eastern Church (1839), question 120.

[68] Cf. e.g. Doe, *Created for Worship*, 230, 231.

REMEMBER, SIN IS *NOT* GOOD

us but it is strangely not natural. We have been dispossessed of where we were, where we *should be*. Yet, it *is* where we *should be*. The worship of the LORD God is true and right, but it also works. It is the way it was designed to be (and thus, not surprisingly, it *works* that way).

We were made for ineffable joy and thus we, naturally, seek for it. The thing about the joy we seek is that it's not quite like our hunger, thirst, or other desires; it cannot be filled within the earth. Therefore, because of our longing, we seek to fill it with that which cannot fill it. We think that, similar to our other "thirsts," it too can be quenched here on earth through tangible means. Yet, experience, many wise people, and Scripture have exhorted us that that is just not the case. There is a greater thirst within us, yet also a greater quenching. There is joy unimaginable, though now not wholly obtainable.

So, hear Romans 6:20-23:

> *For when you were slaves of sin, you were free in regard to righteousness. But what fruit were you getting at that time from the things of which you are now ashamed? For the end of those things is death. But now that you have been set free from sin and have become slaves of God, the fruit you get leads to*

sanctification and its end, eternal life. For the wages of sin is death, but the free gift of God is eternal life in Christ Jesus our Lord.

Thus, sin is not good because it enslaves and leads to death, although it falsely promises life and fulfillment.

SIN'S SOLUTION

In the book of Genesis we read of societal progress. There are advances in technology and the arts. Yet, the problem remains: We have sinful hearts. Thus relationships and, truly, the world remain fractured. Like Humpty Dumpty; we can't put it back together again. The answer to my problem, humanity's problem, and the world's problem is external to us.

Today's problems, like that of all history past, is not solved by advances in technology or even any sort of knowledge or morality. It is solved by a Savior. It is Messiah Jesus that will once and for all eradicate sin and suffering (see e.g. Rom. 11:26-27; Heb. 12:23; 1 Jn. 3:2; Rev. 3:12; 21:1-8, 27; 22:3).

Cartel Land, a recent documentary, is about a group of vigilantes known as the "Autodefensa" who fight Mexican drug cartels. The violent film shows the vicious cycle of corruption that seems impossible to

REMEMBER, SIN IS *NOT* GOOD

break. One of the problems is that evil and sin doesn't stay in the bounds that we assign for it.[69] It is pervasive. It runs through *my heart*. It runs through the vigilantes' hearts. Our final salvation is not in pistols or in politics; it is not finally found in poverty alleviation. It is found in Someone who is outside this whole depraved system. It is found through faith in Messiah Jesus.

When *we* control the measures to make a utopian society the way *we* think it should be, it fails. Whether we control "the stirrings" (e.g. *The Giver*), emotions (e.g. *Equilibrium*), everything (e.g. *The Lego Movie*), or the socioeconomic structure (e.g. *The Hunger Games*) the result is not paradise; it's a sort of hell, at least for many. We messed up utopia; we can't, with our fallible minds, make a new one. Only our Lord can. He has the only infallible and incorruptible mind. He perfectly balances justice and grace. And He alone can make us and all things new.

The recent movie and classic book, *The Giver*, does more than entertain. It teaches us a profound truth, one we would do well to remember: There is no utopian society outside of Christ. We can't fix it. There have been many botched attempts throughout history. They lay dead with their victims.

---

[69] See Emily Belz, "Injustice all around" in *World* July 25, 2015.

REMEMBER, SIN IS *NOT* GOOD

"Everything is awesome. Everything is cool when you're part of a team..." As catchy as *The Lego Movie* song is, it is not exactly right. Everything is *not* awesome, not yet. However, it will be. But not from our own doing (Notice I am not saying we shouldn't work for social justice. We should! Yet, it will not bring the ultimate and forever peace that we long for.).

Heaven *comes down* (Rev. 21:2). We don't, nor can we, build it here. I am with you and Miss America in saying I desire world peace, yet it won't ultimately come until our Lord does. When our Lord comes *He* will wipe away all evil, pain, and tears, not some charismatic leader or government (Rev. 21:1ff). Jesus will make all things new. *Jesus will bring utopia.*

Maranatha! Come Lord Jesus, come!

Sin is not good. But Jesus is. He will bring the shalom we all desire.

> *O' for the worlds that lay asunder,*
> *for the shalom that is slain.*
>
> *We ingrain habits of unrest,*
> *we fester and pass on spoil.*
> *O' for the earth to break,*
> *for all to be made anew.*
>
> *For the habits in my heart to pour out,*
> *and for living waters to ensue.*

REMEMBER, SIN IS *NOT* GOOD

God this world is broken,
we are altogether damaged and
damned.

"Destroy the destroyers of the earth,"
destroy what in me destroys.

Shalom was slain
but through the slain Messiah (is/will
be) renewed.

O' God, Maranatha! (Rev. 22:20)

TAKE AWAY

- Do you understand that "sin is not good"? What impact does/should this have on you?
- Do you see how sin leads to various types of death? How has sin brought "death" to your own life, family, and society?
- Do you realize "you can't have your cake and eat it to?" You can't indulge in sin and not expect it to bring a litany of death.
- How, practically, can you avoid temptation to sin knowing it so often "*looks* good?" (see e.g. Prov. 6:27; Matt. 5:29-30; 18:8-9)
- Think about your sin and how much you don't deserve God's grace. Pray that God would help you know the weight of your sin. Then pray that God

REMEMBER, SIN IS *NOT* GOOD

would help you know that the weight of your sin is cast upon Christ. This is important because those who have been forgiven much, love much (Lk. 7:47).

- Praise God that soon Christ will come and right every wrong. He will banish sin and suffering once and for all. Are you ready? Are you in Christ?

11
"HELLO, MY NAME IS _____ AND I AM ~~AN ADDICT~~ TRANSFORMED"

The Bible does not deny that we were various things—addicts, homosexuals, hateful, prideful, pornographic masturbators—but that is what we *were* (past tense) (1 Cor. 6:9-11; Titus 3:3-5). The emphasis in Scripture is on what we *are* and what we are *called to be*. The Christian does not say, "Hello, my name is ____ and I am an X Y or Z." The Christian says I was dead, but now I am alive. The Christian

"HELLO, MY NAME IS ___ AND I AM AN ADDICT TRANSFORMED"

says I am a struggling sinner, yet I am a saint. The Christians says I am a new creation; I am transformed.

We must remember however that we are "simultaneously saint and sinner." This is the biblical balance. We are holy in Christ and yet we are progressively becoming holy (see 1 Cor. 1:2; Heb. 10:14). I like how John Owen says it: We, who are freed from the condemning power of sin, ought yet to make it our business all our days to kill the indwelling power of sin.[70]

Paul wrote a letter to a church located in Ephesus back in the day. The people there had many struggles. Many of them use to worship various false gods and perhaps were even involved in cult prostitution. But you know what Paul called them when he wrote to them? He called them "God's beautiful creation," "God's masterpiece" (Eph. 2:10). He didn't say, "Now church, make sure that you are constantly reminding yourselves that you were part of the occult. In fact, when you meet together say, 'Hello, my name is ___ and I am an occultist.'" No! He said, "You are new! In Christ! Transformed!"

One of the problems in claiming the identity of "addict," "alcoholic," or "overeater" is that we deny that addiction is a

---

[70] John Owen, *Overcoming Sin and Temptation*, ed. Kelly M Kapic and Justin Taylor (Wheaton: Crossway, 2006), 47, 50.

"HELLO, MY NAME IS ____ AND I AM AN ADDICT TRANSFORMED"

habit that can be finally overcome. I am not saying it won't be a struggle. I am not even saying that it will even finally be overcome in this life. Yet, the Bible teaches the freeing and empowering truth that in Christ we are currently a new creation. It says we are adopted children of God. We are even God's beloved; His treasure.

Labeling may not seem like a big deal but it is. In hospitals it is important for people to be labeled correctly. If someone has a gunshot wound on their leg, they should not be taken to a cardiologist and someone that has the flu, they should not be life-flighted. Labels are important for treatment. Labels are important for our own treatment. The treatment of ourselves. How we look at ourselves, talk to ourselves, think of ourselves.

The Bible talks about sin. Actually, quite a lot about sin. It talks about the deceitfulness of sin, the sin that sticks so closely, our sin natures, and various specific sins among other things. But it does *not* talk about us now being identified as sinner; addict, overeater, alcoholic, or otherwise. Instead, our identity is in Christ and Him alone.

Labeling and identity are not abstract theological concerns. They are practical. We desperately need not just help in life, but a new life. We need transformation. Christ gives us this.

"HELLO, MY NAME IS ____ AND I AM AN ADDICT TRANSFORMED"

So, truly,

> *The scope of recovery is... radically extended within a Christian view of addiction. Indeed 'recovery' does not sufficiently name the Christian hope in the face of addiction. Instead the Christian hopes for 'discovery' and 'new creation'—not a return to some maintainable equilibrium between who we are and what we want but rather a transformation of the self that brings who we are and what we want... into perfect coordination and harmony.*[71]

The Bible doesn't primarily keep us from sin by reminding us what we were when we were dead. It doesn't have us repeat the dreary mantra, "Hello, my name is ____ and I am a(n) ____." And for that I am glad. That is depressing. The Bible instead says things like this:
- Put off your old self, which belongs to your former manner of life and is corrupt through deceitful desires, and... be renewed in the spirit of your minds, and... put on the new self,

---

[71] Kent Dunnington, *Addiction and Virtue: Beyond the Models of Disease and Choice* (Downers Grove: InterVarsity Press, 2011), 183.

"HELLO, MY NAME IS ____ AND I AM AN ADDICT TRANSFORMED"

created after the likeness of God in true righteousness and holiness (Eph. 4:22-23).
- Be imitators of God (Eph. 5:1).
- At one time you were darkness, but now you are light in the Lord. Walk as children of light (Eph. 5:8).

The Bible says we are light in the Lord, a new creation (cf. 2 Cor. 5:17). The Bible says that we are progressively being transformed into the image of God. The Bible says that eternal serenity is available to us in Christ. "The mercies of God work to *forgive* and then to *change* what is deeply evil... Christ's grace slays and replaces (in a lifelong battle) the very lusts that [we have]... We can be fundamentally rewired by the merciful presence of the Messiah"[72]

The Bible has taught me to say, "Hello, my name is Paul and I am transformed." I was a lot of things. But now I am a new creation in Christ.

"Mr. Writer Guy, I believe in Jesus but I don't feel very transformed. I understand that we're simultaneously saint and sinner but my sinner side shows itself a lot more often. I understand that we are holy, right now through Jesus, and yet called to be progressively holy. I, however, am not progressing; or not very much. I feel defeated.

---
[72] Powlison, *Seeing with New Eyes*, 147.

"HELLO, MY NAME IS ____ AND I AM AN ADDICT TRANSFORMED"

I don't feel like saying, 'I am transformed.' I feel like saying 'I am an addict.' So, if I am transformed, can you help me be more transformed? Can you help me in my everyday practice?"

I agree that sometimes it feels like there is a gulf between the fact that we are transformed through Christ and yet called to be transformed. However, it is a biblical truth and, thus, a practical truth. Let's try and see how practical it is.

Very often we respond to our sin with mental punishments. We get wrapped up and warped with stinking thinking. Thinking that is negative and not biblically informed.[73]

When I was younger I remember being greatly discouraged by stinking thinking. I thought because I was wrestling with pornography that I couldn't worship the Lord, I couldn't go to church (or at least enjoy it), I couldn't go to the Lord for help because I was so dirty. My stinking thinking contributed significantly to my depression and hopelessness. My stinking thinking greatly hindered me.

Admittedly, it is difficult to come to the light and have our sin exposed. It can be difficult to go to church and feel overwhelmed with conviction. And yet we all

---

[73] Cf. Heath B. Lambert, *Finally Free: Fighting for Purity with the Power of Grace* (Grand Rapids: Zondervan, 2013), 25.

need the light. We need to have our works exposed (cf. Jn. 3:19-21).

We also need the gospel. We need to remind ourselves that Jesus came for sick sinners. He came to help us, free us. We need to fight against the temptations of stinking thinking and work at kneading gospel truth deep within our core. We need to remind ourselves that our identity, righteousness, and sufficiency are ultimately not grounded in ourselves but in Christ Jesus.

Ephesians teaches us that we're blessed *in* the Beloved, that is, in Christ. If you are a child of God, you don't lose your status... God doesn't un-adopt. When God sees those *in Christ* He says, my beloved son/daughter, in whom I am well pleased (cf. Matt. 3:17; 17:5; Mk. 1:11; 9:7; Lk. 3:22; 20:13; 2 Pet. 1:17). This is not because we are innately good but because Jesus is, and we are united to Him.

The story of the prodigal son is relatable for many of us (see Lk. 15:11-32). Many have left the good provision and company of our Father to seek out a more fulfilling life elsewhere, like in a pig trough. Many of us relate to the son that left. We feel the weight of his foolishness, because it's ours too. However, we must not just focus on the son's actions. That would miss a very important part of the story. We must remember that the father, who represents God the Father, ran to and welcomed his son. He even threw a celebration. Stinking thinking remembers the foolish action but fails to remember the Father that celebrates.

Stinking thinking and mental punishments are not helpful because they are man-centered and self-centered. Instead we need to be Christ-centered. We need to consciously remind ourselves of Christ, what He has done, who we are in union with Him, and the way in which we can be transformed more and more into His image. We need less stinking thinking condemnation and more confession.[74] We need genuine godly sorrow and not just worldly sorrow (note the difference in 2 Cor. 7). We don't need condemnation. We need Christ! We need to focus on Him. Go to Him for help and repentance.

It is crucial that we see the importance of the fact that we are transformed in Christ. This realization helps us focus on Christ and not be self-condemning. It helps us have the necessary endurance to put the "action steps" into action even after we fail. Remember, we are God's "handiwork" (Eph. 2:10) and we are created for good works, yet, we are clearly not saved by them (Eph. 2:8-9).

---

[74] Ibid., 26.

"HELLO, MY NAME IS ____ AND I AM AN ADDICT TRANSFORMED"

TAKE AWAY

- Where do you place your identity? It is easy to think that what is most fundamental to who we are is that we are/were addicts, overeaters, or abused. That is *not* true. While it is true that these things have a significant impact on us they are not what is most fundamental to who we are. These things should not be where we find our identity. We are to find our identity in Christ! He loves us! He died for us. And through Him God—God!—welcomes us in as His beloved and precious child. We are not orphans, castaways, unloved. We are God's artwork. This, my friend, is where we must place our identity and see our significance.
- Pray that God would give you an overwhelming sense of joy over the transformation and new identity that you have received in and through Christ.
- Read 1 Corinthians 6:9-11 (cf. Titus 3:3-5). Paul, here, gives an example list of various sins. Add your own sin to Paul's list in verses 9-10. Maybe for you it's fits of rage, maybe it's substance abuse. Meditate on the fact that left to ourselves, we would have

no hope, we could not inherit the Kingdom of God. That describes our *old ways.* Now, read verse 11, and rejoice! We are *new* and *being made new* through Christ!

12
BE TRANSFORMED BY GOSPEL MOTIVATION

The first "action step" I want to look at is the most important. If this one isn't understood the other ones probably won't see a lot of action. Here's an example from Timothy Keller.

> *Imagine that a baby bird falls from its nest in the sight of a fox. The bird cannot yet fly (hence the fall), but there is a small protective hole at the base of [a] tree that is within a scurry's reach. The fox pounces and sets out after the bird. What should the bird do? Of course, it should scamper into the hole to get out of immediate danger. But if*

BE TRANSFORMED BY GOSPEL MOTIVATION

as time goes on all the bird ever does is scamper, it will never learn what it has been designed for: to fly. And eventually it will surely be eaten by the predators it was designed to escape.

In the short run, we should simply obey God because it is his right and due. But in the long run, the ultimate way to shape our lives and escape the deadly influence of our besetting sins is by moving the heart with the gospel.[75]

So, the first and most important thing we desire is for our heart to be moved and shaped by the gospel. When we have gospel motivation we will be invigorated, energized, and refreshed for transformation. This is what Paul repeatedly prayed for in others (e.g. Eph. 1:15-23; 3:14-21).

The Bible tells us to do a lot of things and not do a lot of things. It tells us to be a certain type of person and not be a certain type of person. But this can be hard. I remember as I kid being told to do something by my mom. And you know what I would say to my mom after she told me to do something? I would say, "Why?" I wanted to know how what I

---

[75] Timothy J. Keller, *Center Church: Doing Balanced, Gospel-centered Ministry in your City* (Grand Rapids: Zondervan, 2012), 70.

BE TRANSFORMED BY GOSPEL MOTIVATION

was doing made sense. Knowing why we are to do something and having motivation to do something is important.

Paul tells the Corinthian church to work hard for the Lord (1 Cor. 15:58). But why? Because Christ has been raised from the dead and they will rise with Him so their faith and their work is not a foolish waste of time but actually makes a lot of sense (cf. 1 Cor. 15:14, 17, 20-22). All over Scripture we are essentially told to be transformed but we are motivated to be transformed by gospel truth (e.g. 1 Kings 8:60-61; 2 Cor. 5:14-15; Eph. 4:1; Col. 3:1-5). So, "we toil and strive because we have our hope set on the living God" (1 Tim. 4:10).

The first "action step" is to be effected and motivated by the gospel. Of course, this is not something we can conjure up on our own. We need the Holy Spirit to work in us. However, it is vital that we give Him fuel to light our souls a flame. So pray as Paul the Apostle did, that God would enlighten your eyes to His truth, that it would effect you deep within (Eph. 1:15-23; 3:14-21). Next, consume God's truth. Read Ephesians and then read it again. Read John Piper's book *Desiring God* or A. W. Tozer's book *The Knowledge of the Holy*, or

BE TRANSFORMED BY GOSPEL MOTIVATION

some other good Christian book that God can use to awaken your soul.[76]

Basically, we desperately need to stoke the fire of our soul. So, stoke your soul! Be transformed by the renewal of your mind (Rom. 12:2)! Here are two Bible verses to meditate on:

> *See what kind of love the Father has given to us, that we should be called children of God; and so we are (1 Jn. 3:1).*
>
> *In love He predestined us for adoption as sons through Jesus Christ, according to the purpose of His will, to the praise of His glorious grace, which He has blessed us in the Beloved (Eph. 1:4b-6).*

What an amazing thing that we, through Christ, are children of God!

However, as J.I. Packer has said,

> *Do I, as a Christian, understand myself? Do I know my own real identity? My own real destiny? I am a child of God. God is my Father; heaven is my home... Say it over and over to yourself first*

---

[76] See Eric L. Johnson, "How God Is Good for the Soul" in *SBJT* 7/4 (Winter 2003).

BE TRANSFORMED BY GOSPEL MOTIVATION

thing in the morning, last thing at night, as you wait for the bus, any time when your mind is free, and ask that you may be enabled to live as one who knows it is all utterly and completely true.[77]

TAKE AWAY

- Pray that God would deeply move you by His love and open your eyes to the amazing truth that through Jesus you are a child of God (see Eph. 1:15-23; 3:14-21).
- Read and memorize Zephaniah 3:17:

  "The LORD your God is in your midst, a mighty one who will save; He will rejoice over you with gladness; He will quiet you by his love; He will exult over you with loud singing."

---

[77] J.I. Packer, *Knowing God* (Downers Grove: InverVarsity Press, 1973), 228.

13
BE TRANSFORMED BY COMMUNITY

The literature on addiction is very clear that social support plays a big part in freedom from addiction. The Bible agrees. Though, of course, it doesn't say it quite like that.

Vital connection to the local expression of Christ's body is very important to our spiritual life. I say "vital connection" because that is what is needed, that is what is so important. It is one thing to go sit in a church gathering and sing songs and hear the pastor proclaim God's truth. It is quite another to know brothers and sisters in the church who can speak truth into your life.

The book of Hebrews tells us to "exhort one another every day, as long as it is called 'today,' that none of you may be hardened by the deceitfulness of sin" (Heb. 3:13). Why is it

BE TRANSFORMED BY COMMUNITY

important that we exhort each other and why is it so important to do it "everyday"? Because if we don't hear from each other in this way it is likely that we will mess up and get tricked by sin's lies; we will be "hardened by the deceitfulness of sin."

It is interesting and sad to me that it seems like Alcoholics Anonymous often does a much better job at this than the church does. This should not be. There are many secular programs that are very good and intentional about helping people. They have realized the importance of "vital connection." So, for instance, some quotes from members of Alcoholics Anonymous:

> *I found my tribe, the social architecture that fulfills my every need of camaraderie and conviviality.*[78]
>
> *A.A. is my home now....I no longer feel alone.*[79]
>
> *The thing that kept me sober until I got a grip on honesty was the love in the room of Alcoholics Anonymous. I made some friends for the first time in my life. Real*

---

[78] *Alcoholics Anonymous* 4th Edition (New York: Alcoholics Anonymous World Services, INC., 2001), 336.

[79] Ibid., 346.

BE TRANSFORMED BY COMMUNITY

friends that cared, even when I was broke and feeling desperate.[80]

"Where am I to find these people to help me in this way?" the Alcoholic Anonymous book asks. It answers,

> *You are going to meet these new friends in your own community... Among them you will make lifelong friends. You will be bound to them with new and wonderful ties, for you will escape disaster together and you will commence shoulder to shoulder your common journey. Then you will know what it means to give of yourself that others may survive and rediscover life. You will learn the full meaning of 'Love thy neighbor as thy self.'[81]*

This should be true of the church. The church should be able to help people in this way. Truly how much more should these things be said of us, we who have the "words of eternal life" (Jn. 6:68); we who know life transforming grace?

In Scripture, we see high importance placed on true sacrificial friendship. We are

---

[80] Ibid.

[81] Ibid., 152

BE TRANSFORMED BY COMMUNITY

to be devoted to serving each other (1 Cor. 16:15; Phil. 2:1-8). In fact, we have a supreme example, we are to love as Jesus loved us (cf. Jn. 15:12-17). We also see that the early church spent much time together (Acts 2:46-47), this is crucial if we are to help each other. Many people involved in A.A. acknowledge this and thus attend meetings once or more every single day. Kent Dunnington says, "The wisdom of the twelve-step program lies in the recognition that the habit of addiction can only be supplanted through the development of another habit that is as pervasive and compelling as the habit of addiction"[82]

Again in Hebrews it says, "Consider," i.e. contemplate, ponder, how to best "stir up one another to love and good works" (Heb. 10:24). This must be an intentional practice. We don't just "let it happen." We ensure that it happens.

Romans 14:19 says "let us pursue what makes for peace and for mutual upbuilding." In Romans too, we see we should intentionally pursue mutual upbuilding. Paul tells Timothy to "flee youthful passions and pursue righteousness, faith, love, and peace, along with those who call on the Lord from a pure heart" (2 Tim. 2:22). Is Timothy supposed to do this all by himself? No! It says

---

[82] Dunnington, *Addiction and Virtue*, 165 cf. 191.

BE TRANSFORMED BY COMMUNITY

"along with those…" From the above verses, and many we did not look at, I think we see the practical, life-protecting, importance of being connected to Christ's body.

We need each other! The secular world in many ways has seen this and the Bible has long since told us this. It reminds us that a cord of three strands is not easily broken (Eccl. 4:12). We need the body of Christ to be the body of Christ. You and I both need this, we need each other! We need vital connection, not mere contact.

So, yes, I want people to come to Sunday morning gatherings but if their involvement stops there then their growth in godliness will be severely limited, if not completely stunted. It is imperative for your health and the health of the church that you are connected, vitally connected, not merely attending.

Relationships are very important in transformation (cf. e.g. Prov. 31:20).

> *While relationships with others are something we do, it is also true that relationships are what we are. We are what our history of relationships has built into us. We need social relationships like the body needs oxygen, but also like stone needs a sculptor to become a work of art (good or bad). We cannot become healthy adult persons*

without relationships. To flourish and to mature into persons of wisdom and Christian virtue, we need the shaping that comes with the best sorts of human relationships. Unfortunately, it is also true that inadequate or dysfunctional interpersonal relationships and interactions can create persons who are not mature and have difficulty flourishing... Whatever we become or are becoming is a matter of both us and others – our actions and others' responses, and our responses to others' actions.[83]

Vital connection, not mere attendance, is vastly important and biblical. There are many "one another" passages that can only be carried out in a small familiar setting. Here is a sampling of the "one another" passages. Think about each of them and about the important place that close friendships have in our lives. It is vital for life, especially our spiritual lives, to practice all the following aspects of life together.

We are to honor one another (Rom. 12:20). We are to accept one another (Rom.

---

[83] Warren S. Brown and Brad D. Strawn, *The Physical Nature of Christian Life* (Cambridge University Press: Kindle Edition, 2012), 72-73.

BE TRANSFORMED BY COMMUNITY

15:7). We are to bear with one another (Eph. 4:2; Col. 3:13). We are to forgive one another (Eph. 4:32; Col. 3:13). We are to pray for one another and confess sins to one another (James 5:16). We are to cheer and challenge one another (Heb. 3:13; 10:24-25). We are to admonish and confront one another (Rom. 15:14; Col. 3:16; Gal. 6:1-6). We are to warn one another (1 Thess. 5:14). We are to teach one another (Col. 3:16). We are to not gossip, slander, or be fake with one another (Gal. 5:15; Rom. 12:9). We are to bear one another's burdens (Gal. 6:2). We are to share possessions with one another (Acts 4:32). We are to submit to one another (Eph. 5:21).

Secular research tells us we need each other. Experience tells us we need each other. The Bible tells us we need each other. If someone falls into sin, then they need loving correction. We need each other. We need brothers and sisters to speak truth into our life (Heb. 3:13).

Sin often starts out small but in the end produces death (cf. James 1:13-15). We need our brothers and sisters in Christ to be on the lookout for us. We need them to be willing to lovingly confront us.

Here is how cancerous sin infects us. Here are the symptoms that must be watched for: The *first* sign is spiritual dullness. *Second* is compromise. *Third* is rationalizing. "It's not that big of a deal," or "I can stop whenever I want," we say to ourselves. *Fourth* is avoidance. This is a very scary step in the process because if the person continues to love darkness rather than light then they will show that they are not of the light (cf. Jn. 3:20-21; 1 Jn. 1:7). The *last step* in the process is exposure. This step, however, requires a brother or sister to lovingly confront the person that has been ensnared by sin. After they have been confronted they can either continue in sin or repent (this procedure is outlined in Matt. 18:15-17).

The truth is that we *all* have the tendency to be hardened by the deceitfulness of sin and at times need the loving rebuke of a brother or sister. This is a grace that God has given to the church. Yes, it is true that we should evaluate our own lives, yet, though redeemed, our hearts have the tendency to try to hide that we are desperately wicked, and thus we welcome the grace of a loving brother or sister's eye.

In Galatians, Paul gives us this helpful exhortation:

> *Brothers [and sisters], if anyone is caught in any transgression, you who are spiritual should restore him in a spirit of gentleness. Keep watch on yourself, lest you too be tempted. Bear one another's burdens, and so fulfill the*

BE TRANSFORMED BY COMMUNITY

law of Christ. For if anyone thinks he is something, when he is nothing, he deceives himself. But let each one test his own work, and then his reason to boast will be in himself alone and not in his neighbor. For each will have to bear his own load (6:1-5).

As we warn others about their sin, we must remember a few things:
1. We must guard *ourselves* against temptation (Gal. 6:1).
2. We need others in our lives and they need us (v. 2)
3. We must remember that we are not above sin and we must not be prideful (v. 3).
4. We should test *ourselves* (v. 4a). In the language of Jesus, we should make sure there is no log in our eye while we seek to remove the speck from someone else's (Matt. 7:5).
5. Finally, we see that we must ensure that we are doing our part in helping others with their sin (Gal. 6:2, 5).

So, after we have done all of the above and made sure that our motives are pure and restorative then what? The *first* step to restore brothers and sisters in Christ is to accept that it is our responsibility to do so. *Second*, we act in gentleness (Gal. 5:1). *Third*, it is good to use the Bible when correcting someone. When possible just showing them a few verses to read can be helpful. This allows the Spirit to work on them and it also shows that you do not come to them on your own authority. However, at times it is not that simplistic. *Fourth*, we must focus on the correct goal: restoration.

We are told in Scripture to bear one another's burdens (Gal. 6:1-5). Bearing one another's burdens requires nearness.[84] In my short life, I have born a lot of burden, i.e. helped a lot of people move. I think I've helped one of my sisters move 6 times.

I've also had a lot of people help me. When I moved into my current place, something like 30 youth showed up to help. It was fun. It was wild.

The point is, if we are going to bear burdens or have help with our burdens we must be near and involved. When I moved to Ohio the 30 youth didn't help me. Because they were in Virginia and I hadn't met them yet. We need to be in a community to receive help from a community. We need to be in a community to help those in the community.

Be vitally connected to the local expression of Christ's body and bride the

---

[84] Cf. Thabiti Anyabwhile, *The Life of God in the Soul of the Church: The Root and Fruit of Spiritual Fellowship* (Fearn, Scotland: Christian Focus Publications, 2012), 120-21.

church. The church needs you and you need the church.

TAKE AWAY

- Are you involved in a local church, not just attending?
- Are you up front and honest with your trusted church friends so they can help you? Are you willing to lovingly confront and be confronted?
- Ensure that you are practicing the five steps outlined above when you confront someone with their sin.

14
BE TRANSFORMED BY RADICAL MEASURES

Various texts on recovery from addiction say that maintaining abstinence or sobriety requires avoiding triggers. Triggers are different for different people but they can include places, friends, and emotions. We must avoid our triggers as much as we can. We must also develop biblical and healthy way to handle life's stressors. The Bible teaches us that we are to take radical steps to avoid sin, we should avoid "triggers" (see Matt. 5:29-30; 18:8-9).

I've always hated buddy rushes.

"Buddy rushes? What's that?"

Buddy rushes are a form of military movement under enemy fire. It is a movement used to advance on the enemy. When under enemy fire it is important to

BE TRANSFORMED BY RADICAL MEASURES

have cover and concealment. And it is important to move quickly. Here is how the buddy rush works:

> *Step 1: "Buddy, got me covered?" (Buddy #1) – Ensures that he has cover from enemy fire*
>
> *Step 2: "Got you covered!" (Buddy #2) – Puts lead down range*
>
> *Step 3: "I'm up, he sees me, I'm down." (Buddy #1) – Moves forward as fast as possible and takes cover*
>
> *Step 4: "Buddy, got me covered?" (Buddy #2) – Ensures that he has cover from enemy fire*
>
> *Step 5: "Got you covered!" (Buddy #1) – Puts lead down range*
>
> *Step 6: "I'm up, he sees me, I'm down." (Buddy #2) – Ensures that he has cover from enemy fire*
>
> *Repeat as needed.*

As you can see the whole process seems pretty silly. I do not really enjoy calling anyone "buddy." And I certainly don't enjoy

BE TRANSFORMED BY RADICAL MEASURES

sprinting for as long as it takes me to say "I'm up, he sees me, I'm down" and then crashing headlong into the ground behind some tree or rock. To be honest with you the whole routine is tiring and I don't enjoy it.

You know what, though? My opinion of the buddy rush would be radically altered if I was in combat under enemy fire. I would not think it was silly at all! It would be absolutely necessary.

When the situation is life and death it, changes our perspective. Things that would have otherwise been silly become necessary.

It is the same way when it comes to fighting sin. When we realize our fight against sin is life or death we will take extreme precautions and radical measures but it will not seem odd or silly. It will simply be necessary. What we do. So, the first priority here is to realize that the enslaving sin you are fighting will kill you so you must avoid it at all costs. Jesus said, "If your eye causes you to sin, tear it out and throw it away." Why would anyone do that? Because, Jesus responds, "It is better for you to enter life with one eye than with two eyes to be thrown into the hell of fire" (Matt. 18:9). So, Jesus is saying, sin is that serious.

The second step, avoid sin at all costs (i.e. "tear out your eye"). This is a very biblical teaching and secular programs have caught on to it as well (though, of course, they would

BE TRANSFORMED BY RADICAL MEASURES

not use the three-letter word sin. The Scriptures teach that Satan is like a roaring lion seeking someone to devour. How do we respond to a fierce lion that wants to eat us? We stay clear. We resist him, firm in our faith. We're sober-minded and watchful (1 Peter 5:8-9).

Because sin is so serious and so deathly we must also avoid the people, places, and things that would tempt us to sin. (Prov. 4:14-15; 13:20; 23:19-20; 1 Cor. 5:11 cf. Prov. 7). We must take extreme precautions because whatever our temptation is, it is appealing and alluring, however, in the end it "is bitter as wormwood, sharp as a two-edged sword" (Prov. 5:4) and leads to death (Prov. 5:5).

How do we avoid temptation? What does this look like? I know godly men that refuse to have a smartphone because that phone, with all its helpful apps, will become, in their hands, a bomb. An explosive that will sever their heart with sinful lust. They refrain from what for many people is harmless because they know, for them, it is a death wish.

So also, for you. Maybe you can have a smartphone but maybe you can't have access to your car keys because if you do you will gamble everything away. Whatever the exact application for you, you must be sure you are taking radical measures to avoid temptation.

BE TRANSFORMED BY RADICAL MEASURES

"Put on the Lord Jesus Christ, and make no provision for the flesh, to gratify its desires" (Rom. 13:14).

We are not merely to 'stop trying and start trusting'; we must seek to discipline our bodies and bring them under subjection (1 Cor. 9:24 cf. Col. 3:5; 2 Peter 3:14). Or course, neither are we to "start trying and stop trusting." We must *try* and *trust* with all we are. We must work out our own salvation with fear and trembling for it is God who works in us (Phil. 2:12-13). I have a friend that has said, "God can move a mountain but we have to bring a shovel."[85]

A farmer is not free to think he will have a good harvest unless he picks up the shovel and jumps on the tractor and does the hard and intentional work day in and day out. However, as hard as he works and as responsible as he is for the growth and cultivation of his field, he cannot in himself bring a successful harvest.

The farmer is *responsible* and *dependent*. He must do work. He must also trust. Trust that the seed will germinate. Trust that the sun will shine and the rains will come.

Just as the farmer would have no crop apart from work, so we will have no holiness

---

[85] Sanctification is God's work (1 Thess. 5:23; Eph. 5:26; Phil. 1:6; Titus 2:14; Heb. 13:20-21) and ours (Phil. 2:12-13; Rom. 8:13; 12:1-2; 9; 16-17).

BE TRANSFORMED BY RADICAL MEASURES

without work. But just as the farmer would have no crop apart from the God's work, we will have not holiness without God's work.[86]

We must be like the farmer. We must work. And we must trust.

Eating healthy involves two things. First, not eating certain things that are bad for us. Second, making a deliberate effort to eat other things that are good for us.

A "spiritual diet" also involves at least two things. On the one hand, it means not doing some things, or thinking on certain things, that will harm us. This could include movies and TV shows, the music we listen to, or the friends we hang out with. On the other hand, it means doing some things that will benefit us, so that we are in a better position to know God's will. This is where the spiritual discipline of Bible reading, prayer, church, being with other Christians, etc. comes in.[87]

As we strive after holiness, we must behold the LORD's holiness. We must trust God and pray that we would not be led into temptation but be delivered from the evil one (Luke 11:4; 22:40; Heb. 4:16). We must put off the old and put on the new (Eph. 4:22-24; Rom. 12:1-2; Col. 3). We must work with all

---

[86] Jerry Bridges, *In the Pursuit of Holiness* (Colorado Springs: NavPress, 1996), 9.

[87] Adapted from Dave DeKlavon class notes on "Interpreting Romans" (Louisville, Ky.: Boyce College, 2010).

BE TRANSFORMED BY RADICAL MEASURES

the power that He so powerfully works within us to kill sin (Col. 1:29; Phil. 2:12-13; 1 Cor. 12:6; Heb. 13:21; 1 Cor. 15:10). We must practice radical amputation (Matt. 5:27-30). We must set our eyes on Christ and thus be transformed into His image (Col. 3:2).

Jerry Bridges sums it up well for us. "Truly the choice is ours. What will we choose? Will we accept our responsibility and discipline ourselves to live in habitual obedience to the will of God? Will we persevere in the face of frequent failure, resolving never to give up?"[88]

TAKE AWAY

- Do you know how serious your sin is? Until you know the seriousness of sin you won't see the importance of taking radical measures to avoid it.
- Take the necessary, even radical, steps to avoid what will lead you into sin. Kill sin or it will kill you!
- Put the proper accountability in place. If you're struggling with pornography don't allow yourself to know the password to your computer, put someone in place to moderator the sites you visit, or simply don't ever use the internet. Taking extreme

---

[88] Bridges, *In the Pursuit of Holiness*, 156-57.

BE TRANSFORMED BY RADICAL MEASURES

measures will be different for different people. However, the common principle that applies across the board is that we all must put structures in place that will help us fight sin. Of course, in all of this, our foremost desire is not just the avoidance of sin but the hatred of sin.

15
BE TRANSFORMED BY WORSHIP

If we understand our obsession/addiction to be a form of idolatry we must work at fostering worship of the one *true* God. We must fight against the lie that says porn or substances will give us superior satisfaction. [89] God is the creator of all good gifts. He spread out the universe like a blanket. We can't find ultimate satisfaction in God's gifts, especially when deformed and defiled. We can find true life-giving satisfaction in God alone. We must fight our enslaving sin with the consistent cannon fire of satisfaction in God.

---

[89] Cf. John Piper, *Future Grace* (Sisters, OR: Multnomah Publishers, 1995), 336.

BE TRANSFORMED BY WORSHIP

How do we do this? There are various ways but perhaps the biggest thing is purposely think on God's truth[90] and singing gospel songs in community (cf. Jn. 15:1-11; Eph. 5:17-21; Col. 3:15-17). Therefore, instead of *nibbling* on what the latest self-help book has to offer we must *feast* on Scripture. We must look to the true God to satisfy our every need.

I was looking at some "before and after pictures" of meth addicts today. It is haunting and sad. I can only think of Romans 1:18-32. When we deny God and look for satisfaction in other things we become less human. We reflect His image less and less. Sin is counterintuitive. It can look so good, so alluring, "but in the end it is bitter as wormwood, sharp as a two-edged sword" (Prov. 5:4).

Thus,

> *Far from the belief that Christians have to give up everything they enjoy to do dreary things, the truth is that your pleasure mechanism is rearranged. You are freed to feel all sorts of exquisite joys you never imagined. It takes less and less effort. In the stained pleasure cycle, the addictive cycle, it takes more and*

---
[90] Ibid., 335.

BE TRANSFORMED BY WORSHIP

more to push the lever of joy. Stained pleasures have this corroding effect: They always up the ante.[91]

Jesus never sinned. He never indulged in so much of what Hollywood and this world sells as pleasure. And yet, Jesus had more joy than anyone who ever walked the face of this earth. Jesus was no Stoic either. He felt pain. Great pain. Beyond what I can comprehend. Yet He had a constant unceasing joy. In fact, His joy was so great that it preserved Him through His agony on the cross (Heb. 12:2).

It should be said as well, that Jesus was not a killjoy. He turned water into wine. Jesus was not afraid of appropriately celebrating with friends and family. Jesus knew joy and pleasure. Jesus took joy and pleasure in beautiful sunsets, friendships, and food. But His all persevering joy was taken in His relationship with God His Father. All else could be stripped away but with that remaining He was content.

Paul and the other Apostles were willing to give up all. Why? Because Jesus is worth it! And nothing else is. As Paul said, everything is trash, refuse, compared to Christ! Truly, as Jim Elliot said and now intimately knows, "he

---

[91] David Powlison, *Breaking the Addictive Cycle: Deadly Obsessions or Simple Pleasures?* (Greensboro, NC: New Growth Press, 2010), 17.

is no fool who gives what he cannot keep to gain what he cannot lose."

Even our most sublime experiences of worship pale in comparison to what awaits us. Worship here is a mere foretaste. "What no eye has seen, nor ear heard, what God has prepared for those who love Him" (1 Cor. 2:9 cf. Ps. 67; Matt. 25:34; Rom. 8:32).

Even creation, though fallen, points to profound shalom. We've all, I'm sure, had moments that are profoundly joyous and surreal. Those moments, those brief moments, are a whisper of a distant reality. Images captured by National Geographic help us recall from where we fell. There are combinations of colors and landscapes even now that portray wonder.

Notice also that if God has made all good, all the good things we so enjoy, surely He can and does heap good upon good. As Jonathan Edwards has said,

> *God is infinitely the greatest being, so He is allowed to be infinitely the most beautiful and excellent. And all the beauty to be found throughout the whole creation is but the reflection of the diffused beams of that Being who hath an infinite fullness of brightness and glory...*

BE TRANSFORMED BY WORSHIP

God is not only infinitely greater and more excellent than all other beings, but He is the head of the universal system of existence; the foundation and fountain of all being and all beauty; from whom all is perfectly derived, and on whom all is most absolutely and perfectly dependent; of whom, and through whom, and to whom is all being and all perfection; and whose being and beauty is as it were the sum and comprehension of all existence and excellence: much more than the sun is the fountain and summary comprehension of all the light and brightness of the day.[92]

The One who formed all things is our portion (Jer. 51:19)! There is no better inheritance. There is nothing better. An impoverished and stricken orphan adopted by Gates or Rockefeller does not have the ability to understand. God is a perpetual fountain of life, peace, joy, and truly enumerable other gifts.

Jesus, as the third person of the Trinity, is infinitely the greatest being. Yet Jesus is also

---

[92] Jonathan Edwards, "The Nature of True Virtue," 550-551 in *Ethical Writings*, Ed. Paul Ramsey, *The Works of Jonathan Edwards, Vol. 8* (New Haven: Yale University Press, 1989).

BE TRANSFORMED BY WORSHIP

the good King. A King that would serve, suffer, and die for His servants. He is a perfect King that gives a Kingdom of eternal and perfect peace. We don't have the ability to understand His glory and the ensuing peace and prosperity that He'll bring.

We're amazingly shortsighted if we seek our final good and pleasure here. C. S. Lewis was good at speaking to this truth. He reminds us that there are many great promises of reward in the Bible. Our problem is not so much that our desires are too strong, but that they're too weak, and directed to the wrong things. We are a fickle bunch. We get distracted with lesser pleasures. We're like a small child so focused on consuming lima beans that we don't pay attention to the offer of ice cream.[93]

As Christians, we must not listen to the lies of this world, the lies of Satan. We must not be shortsighted. We must not believe that this world offers us better pleasure, better joy. It is simply not true.

Hear, pray, and believe God's Word: God, You make known to me the path of life; in Your presence there is fullness of joy; at Your

---

[93] See C. S. Lewis, *The Weight of Glory, and Other Addresses* (New York: Collier, 1980), 3-4.

BE TRANSFORMED BY WORSHIP

right hand are pleasures forevermore (Ps. 16:11).[94]

"Path of life." How true that statement is! There is a way that seems right to a man, as the Proverb says, but in the end it is the way to death (Prov. 14:12; 16:25). Surely, I didn't distinguish between the path of life and path of death. It was God's grace. He made known to me... He gave the lamp to light my feet (cf. Ps. 119:105). Certainly by myself I was lost and trudging down the path of destruction. However, it's not just me. This is true of all of us.

Where does this new path, this path of life, lead? To "fullness of joy!" And this happens in God's presence. This indeed makes logical sense since God created all things good. Yet, the text doesn't merely say "pleasure." It doesn't just say pleasure because pleasure is not substantive enough. Joy, or *shalom*, is deep and abiding unlike the fleeting nature of pleasure, here one minute, gone the next. So, the text says, "pleasures forevermore." And note that it's not just joy, it's the "fullness of joy." Joy is not lacking in any sense before God almighty! Joy overflows. In the new creation we will swim

---

[94] Eric Johnson says, "The infinitely joyful God is alone capable of supplying human blessedness, because he alone is filled with overflowing blessedness" (*Foundations of Soul Care*, 43).

BE TRANSFORMED BY WORSHIP

in joy, it will perpetually be all around us, it will engulf us.

Notice again that this path leads to real life and not the fleeting pleasures that promise so much yet return so little—a short-lived smile and death. No, this new path—path to God!—leads to "pleasures forevermore."

The path that we were on led to pleasure—but it also led to death. The path that God graciously puts us on leads to joy, forever pleasure, to Himself!

Who gives us this path of life? In whose presence is fullness of joy? Where do we find pleasures forevermore? The LORD God! Not pot. Not sex. Not drugs. None of those things (see Ps. 73:25; 84:10).

The book of Ecclesiastes reminds us that "there is no *shalom* in our hearts, and there is no *shalom* in the offerings of this world. We are cursed; creation is cursed. We are groaning; creation is groaning. The ache is bigger than all of us."[95] Solomon, who must have been some odd mix of Steve Jobs, Bill Gates, and Justin Timberlake,[96] would exhort us not to waste our strength or time seeking for our ultimate fulfillment in this earth. It's pointless to do that! Enjoy the good gifts, he

---

[95] Matt Chandler, *The Explicit Gospel* (Wheaton: Crossway, 2012), 133.

[96] Cf. Ibid., 124.

BE TRANSFORMED BY WORSHIP

would say, but don't find ultimate shalom here, *you can't.*

It is only through our Messiah and Savior Jesus that we can have *true* and *lasting* shalom.

So, LORD, Satisfy us at all times with your steadfast love (Ps. 90:14). God help us to taste and see that You are good. Help us to invest in the joys in heaven and lay aside ungodly pleasures here.

> *We have eternity in our hearts.*
> *We cry out like two daughters: Give and Give.*
> *The fire of our soul won't be quenched or squelched.*
> *It burns on,*
> *consumes all,*
> *and is left*
> *empty.*
>
> *Empty abyss,*
> *blank, black hole.*
> *We suck in stars, oceans, all;*
> *and yet repine.*
>
> *Yes, my soul's an arid land.*
> *An empty dry sponge.*
> *It sucks up all it can,*
> *yet remains coarse and craving.*
>
> *My soul's a vacuum*
> *that won't be filled.*

All is engulfed,
yet I'm left empty.

We have eternity in our hearts
and can only be filled with the Eternal.

We have an infinite longing
that is only meant by the Infinite.

Our cavernous soul is only filled
by the LORD.

We can only be sated
by our Savior.

Our repining will finally wane
when we stand on heaven's plane.

Our soul's fallowed ground
will burst with new life.

Our bottomless shaft
will abound in streams of joy.

TAKE AWAY

- Pray that God would satisfy you with the joy that only He can provide. In fact, pray and memorize Psalm 16:11: "You make known to me the path of life; in your presence there is fullness of joy; at your right hand are pleasures forevermore." Ask God to use this verse to recalibrate your thinking.

BE TRANSFORMED BY WORSHIP

- Do you understand and believe that God as the good Creator and Lord of the universe can give you the true and lasting shalom you seek? And do you understand and believe that all Satan has to offer is a defective and damning façade of what's actually true and good?
- Intentionally "set your minds on things that are above, not on things that are on earth" (Col. 3:2 see also Phil. 4:8). Expand the number of things that excite your *holy* longing. Enjoy art, landscapes, novels, poetry, friendships, etc. that arouse godly desire for sheer goodness and the One who is its overflowing fountain of all goodness.[97]
- Be intentional about pursuing the LORD in worship. Taking in God's Word is especially important here. It reshapes our desires and makes us fall in line with His truth. So, instead of listening to the lies that the media sells, through magazines, movies, and the like, we need to be shaped by right priorities. We need our ideal of

---

[97] See Cornelius Plantiga Jr., *Engaging God's World: A Christian Vision of Faith, Learning, and Living* (Grand Rapids: Eerdmans, 2002), 7.

prospering reshaped by what really matters.

16
BE TRANSFORMED BY A NEW CONSUMING PASSION

A CONSUMING LIFE PASSION?

Instead of feening for a substance or porn, we need to have a new and better all-consuming passion. We need to have a new purpose with a new goal as its end. We need a reason to get out of bed in the morning. We need a reason to be.

One of the fundamental questions that psychologists face is what is to be the motivational force in our lives? Is it to get rich? Propagate our genes? To enjoy as much pleasure as we can? What is to be the fuel for the engine of our lives? Do we have anything that can propel us through the sufferings and struggles of life?

This question cries out to be answered, and how it's answered will have profound implications on the way that we live. Many, I'm sure, are unaware of their motivations and could care less about them. However, that this is a great mistake.

The athlete, for instance, competes for a prize and is very much aware of what that prize is. We, like the athlete, must not only be aware that there is a prize but what that prize is. We must seek to live with the intentionality of an athlete.

An athlete will discipline their body and bring it under subjection in pursuit of the prize. And when focused on the prize the athlete will gladly do away with hindrances. However, the athlete must have a goal, be competing for a prize, and have an idea of what that prize is if they are to have motivation to compete well.

CHRISTIANS HAVE MOTIVATION TO "COMPETE"

The language of running the race and competing for a prize were frequently used by the Apostle Paul. He was someone that clearly had a reason for getting out of bed in

BE TRANSFORMED BY A NEW CONSUMING PASSION

the morning. He had a consuming passion. He said, "I count everything as absolutely worthless compared to Christ." Paul suffered the loss of all things in order that he could gain Christ. We also see that Jesus Himself raced the race and endured the cross for the joy that was set before Him (Heb. 12:1-2)

We too need motivation. We need to be motivated like the Apostle Paul. We need the love of Christ to be the fuel that burns and propels us through the sufferings and struggles of life. Christ alone is sufficient motivation. Christ Jesus, as the Apostle Paul, Augustine, and many others make clear, alone satisfies and is worth living for.

The end of the last book of the Bible, the book of Revelation, tells us in chapter 21 what our ultimate goal is. To see God face to face, to be in the eternal temple where He will make all things new. Where He will wipe away every tear from our eye. Where there will be no more pain or crying anymore. Where we will have pleasure forevermore in His presence.

So we see that we have much that God has called us to do. We have much purpose. We have a reason to *be*. We would do well to set God's truth before us so that we are motivated to live for the prize.

A verse that God has used to wake me up to the unseen realities and motivate me to purposeful living to His glory is 1 Corinthians

BE TRANSFORMED BY A NEW CONSUMING PASSION

15:58. It says, "Therefore, my beloved brothers, be steadfast, immovable, always abounding in the work of the Lord, knowing that your labor in the Lord is not in vain." This verse, when understood in the context of chapter 15, shows us that it makes sense for us to be motivated to labor for the Lord because of the reality of the resurrection of Jesus.

The Bible verse that says, "Whether you eat or drink, whatever you do, do you all to the glory of God" (1 Cor. 10:31) is not just a Bible verse. It is not just a good tagline under the name of some private Christian school. It is the way that it makes sense for us to live in light of the glorious gospel. In a similar way, the oft-quoted phrase "our chief end [or main purpose in life] is to glorify God and enjoy him forever" is not a mere tagline but a phrase that gets at a biblical motivational reality.

The Bible is not beyond logic. It tells us what is logical. How it makes sense to live. The Bible says if God is God then live for Him (1 Kings 18:21). It just makes good sense. The Bible tells us that it is logical for us to offer ourselves and our entire lives to God in worship because His love and grace are so amazing (Rom. 12:1-2).

If the Bible and the gospel are true, as I believe them to be, then it makes complete logical sense for us to live completely for the

Lord. However, we need to work at reminding ourselves of this logical truth.

We need to work at intentionally motivating ourselves with biblical truth. Otherwise we will wander purposeless and lethargic through life. "Boredom" also "arises in the context of a lack of purpose and passion. If we feel no interest in the world around us and don't know where we're going, we will feel empty and restless. And that restlessness can propel us into desperate, unwise attempts at finding pleasure."[98]

So, let's do some homework and create a biblically informed purpose statement.

TAKE AWAY: CREATE YOUR OWN MOTIVATIONAL PURPOSE STATEMENT

We have laid a little bit of groundwork. Now it's your turn. I want you to write out a biblically informed motivational purpose statement for your life (consider e.g. 1 Tim. 6:11-12; 1 Cor. 6:18-20; 9:24-27; 15:58; Gal. 6:8-10; 1 Pet.1:13-19; 5:8-11; Heb. 12:1-2).

Just write something down. It does not have to be able to stand the test of time like the Westminster Shorter Catechism on your first attempt. Your purpose statement can

---

[98] Dan B. Allender & Tremper Longman III, *Breaking the Idols of Your Heart: How to Navigate the Temptations of Life* (Downers Grove: IVP Books, 2007), 104-05.

BE TRANSFORMED BY A NEW CONSUMING PASSION

adapt and grow as you do. You can be more thorough later but for now jot something down right here in the book.

My own purpose statement is not the best and I certainly could do better about purposely keeping it in my head so that it will be lived out through my hands. However, the purpose behind the statement is not to make it timeless or flawless. It is to be purposeful about our purpose. We have a purpose and it is great. We have a reason to wake up in the morning. A reason to be. I reason to say no to whatever sin it is that calls our name.

_____
_____
_____
_____
_____
_____
_____
_____

(NOT A) CONCLUSION

This is not a conclusion because you are *not* done. The process of sanctification is not quick. People want their problems, their addiction, their sin, to be taken away right away. They want fast food. They want to use the microwave but it's more like a crockpot. It takes a while. But in the end it's worth it.

There are many other things we could talk about and I would like to talk about but as I have said "there's no silver bullet." We must simply go on trusting Jesus and fight the gospel-centered war.

Keep up the fight! Press on. Seek the Lord! Follow hard after Him. Always remember His abundant transforming grace.

Don't forget, we must minister to those with enslaving addiction problems, body and soul. We must remember the main problem is the heart problem. However, we must not leave out the physical component. We must seek to minister to the whole person, remembering that there is no "cookie cutter mold," but that each

(NOT A) CONCLUSION

individual must be ministered to as an individual. This will not be an easy thing and will take much prayer, biblical wisdom, and the help of the church community, but by the grace of God addicts, whatever type of addicts, can be successful in their battle against addiction.

> *"Now may our Lord Jesus Christ Himself, and God our Father, who loved us and gave us eternal comfort and good hope through grace, comfort your hearts and establish them in every good work and word."*
> – 2 Thessalonians 2:16-17

ABOUT THE AUTHOR

Paul O'Brien grew up in an old farmhouse in Ohio with 9 siblings. He married his childhood sweetheart, has 3 children, served in the military 9 years, and has been in pastoral ministry for 7 years. You will find Paul reading, writing, and watching extreme sports with his family in his spare time.

Paul oversees the youth ministry at Sovereign Grace Church in Fairfax, VA. He is currently pursuing his M.Div. in Christian Ministry from SBTS and he received his B.A. in Expository Preaching and Pastoral Leadership from Boyce College.

He resides in Fairfax, VA with his wife, Leah, and three children.

Connect with Paul:
Blog: newcreationinx.org
Twitter: @newcreationinX

CPSIA information can be obtained
at www.ICGtesting.com
Printed in the USA
LVOW04s2335160516
488553LV00037B/930/P

9 780692 684863